VIETNAMESE *VEGAN*

Publisher: Taste of Vegan
Printed in the USA
Year: 2023

The information contained within this book is for educational and informational purposes only. The author and publisher assume no responsibility for any errors or omissions in the content herein. The content is not intended to be a substitute for professional dietary or medical advice. Readers are advised to consult their healthcare providers or qualified professionals regarding dietary choices, nutritional information, and individual health concerns.

Introduction

Ladies and gentlemen, fellow food lovers, and culinary adventurers, I extend to you a warm and fragrant welcome to the "Vietnamese Vegan Cookbook." As we embark on this flavorful journey through the heart of Vietnamese cuisine, I want to take a moment to share the essence of what this culinary voyage is all about.

The Cookbook's Theme: In the realm of plant-based cooking, Vietnamese cuisine stands as a beacon of balance, flavor, and tradition. This cookbook is a tribute to the vibrant and diverse world of Vietnamese flavors, reimagined through the lens of vegan ingredients. It's an invitation to savor the rich tapestry of Vietnam's culinary heritage while embracing a compassionate and sustainable way of eating.

Inspiration Behind the Cookbook: The inspiration for creating this cookbook was born from a deep appreciation for Vietnamese food, a cuisine that celebrates fresh herbs, aromatic spices, and the harmonious interplay of flavors. It's also rooted in a desire to make these culinary treasures accessible to all, irrespective of dietary choices. Vietnam's culinary legacy is a gift to the world, and we wanted to ensure that everyone could partake in its delicious offerings.

What to Expect: Within these pages, you'll find over 100 plant-based recipes that span the full spectrum of Vietnamese cuisine. From soul-warming soups to tantalizing spring rolls, aromatic stir-fries to mouthwatering noodle dishes, we've captured the essence of Vietnamese breakfast, lunch, and dinner, all made easy with simple-to-find ingredients. Alongside these recipes, you'll discover vivid photographs that not only showcase the dishes but also transport you to the bustling streets and bustling markets of Vietnam.

So, my fellow culinary explorers, prepare to embark on a journey that will awaken your taste buds, deepen your appreciation for the art of Vietnamese cooking, and open a world of plant-based possibilities. As we delve into each recipe, we'll unravel the stories and flavors that make Vietnamese cuisine a true culinary gem.

But enough preamble; let's dive right in. The vibrant world of Vietnamese vegan delights awaits, and I'm delighted to have you by my side as we explore its many wonders. Welcome to the "Vietnamese Vegan Cookbook." Let's savor every moment and every bite of this flavorful adventure together.

Cooking Philosophy or Approach

Welcome, my fellow food enthusiasts, to the aromatic world of the "Vietnamese Vegan Cookbook." Here, amidst the pages filled with plant-based treasures, we delve into not just recipes, but an entire approach to cooking and savoring the art of Vietnamese cuisine.

1. The Heart of Freshness: In Vietnamese cooking, freshness reigns supreme. We celebrate vibrant herbs, crisp vegetables, and ingredients picked at the peak of ripeness. It's a philosophy that infuses each dish with an explosion of flavors and textures, a philosophy that invites you to explore the local markets and embrace seasonal produce.

2. The Art of Balance: Vietnamese cuisine is a delicate dance of flavors. The balance of sweet, salty, sour, and spicy is the essence of every dish. We use ingredients like fish sauce (although vegan alternatives are embraced here), lime, and chili to create harmonious symphonies on the palate.

3. The Power of Simplicity: While Vietnamese cuisine is known for its complexity of flavors, simplicity in preparation is a guiding principle. We use few ingredients, but each one plays a significant role. It's about letting the natural taste of the ingredients shine through, unburdened by heavy sauces or overwrought seasonings.

4. A Symphony of Herbs: Fresh herbs are the heart and soul of Vietnamese cooking. Cilantro, mint, basil, and Thai basil are like culinary brushes, painting each dish with bursts of freshness. Their use is liberal, and they elevate even the simplest of dishes.

5. Homemade Goodness: In Vietnamese kitchens, homemade is the gold standard. From rich, aromatic broths for soups to hand-rolled spring rolls, we cherish the process of creating from scratch. It's a labor of love that's both rewarding and soul-nourishing.

6. The Power of Tofu: Tofu is the vegan hero in Vietnamese cuisine. It's a versatile canvas that absorbs the flavors of the dishes it's cooked in. We treat it with reverence, whether it's sizzling in a stir-fry, simmering in a soup, or gracing a fresh salad.

7. A Love for Pho-nomenal Soups: Pho, the iconic Vietnamese noodle soup, is a culinary emblem of our culture. We pay homage to its intricate flavors and soothing warmth with vegan versions that capture the essence of this beloved dish.

8. The Joy of Family and Community: Vietnamese cuisine is deeply rooted in the tradition of sharing meals with loved ones. It's about gathering around a table, passing dishes, and savoring the bonds that food creates. This cookbook embraces that spirit, inviting you to create these cherished moments with your own community.

In the "Vietnamese Vegan Cookbook," we embark on a journey that celebrates the vibrant, nourishing, and soul-satisfying flavors of Vietnam. It's a journey that invites you to embrace freshness, balance, and simplicity while savoring the joy of creating and sharing meals. As we explore these recipes together, I hope you find inspiration, connection, and the pure delight of Vietnamese vegan cuisine.

Vegan Canh Bún (Rice Noodle Soup)
See Page 48

Tips for Successful Cooking

Welcome to the vibrant world of Vietnamese cuisine, my fellow culinary enthusiasts. As we navigate the tantalizing pages of the "Vietnamese Vegan Cookbook," I'd like to share some essential tips and techniques that will elevate your plant-based Vietnamese culinary adventures to new heights. Let's dive into the art of successful cooking.

1. Balance of Flavors: Vietnamese cuisine is renowned for its harmony of flavors – sweet, sour, salty, bitter, and umami. When preparing your dishes, aim to strike a balance between these elements. Taste as you go, and adjust the seasonings to create a symphony of tastes in every bite.

2. Fresh Ingredients are Key: In Vietnamese cooking, fresh herbs and produce are the stars of the show. Seek out the freshest ingredients you can find, whether it's aromatic herbs like cilantro and Thai basil, crisp vegetables, or ripe tropical fruits. Freshness is the secret ingredient that brings authenticity to your dishes.

3. The Art of Nuoc Mam: Fish sauce, or nuoc mam, is a staple in Vietnamese cuisine. To achieve that unmistakable umami depth, replace fish sauce with a vegan alternative like soy sauce or mushroom sauce. Experiment with different options to find the one that suits your taste best.

4. Mastering Rice Noodles: Rice noodles are a cornerstone of Vietnamese dishes like pho and bun cha. To prepare them perfectly, soak them in warm water until they become pliable, then cook briefly in boiling water until tender. Rinse with cold water to stop the cooking process and prevent clumping.

5. The Power of Lemongrass: Lemongrass is a quintessential Vietnamese ingredient that imparts a citrusy, aromatic flavor. To use it, remove the tough outer layers and finely mince the tender white inner part. It adds a bright, refreshing note to your dishes.

6. Embrace Rice Paper Rolls: Rice paper rolls, or goi cuon, are a delightful and healthy Vietnamese snack or appetizer. To work with rice paper, dip each sheet briefly in warm water until pliable, then fill with your choice of ingredients. Roll tightly, tucking in the sides as you go, for a perfect, translucent roll.

7. Slow Simmering Soups: Vietnamese soups like pho and bun rieu require slow simmering to develop complex flavors. Patience is key. Allow your broths to infuse with herbs and spices over time, and you'll be rewarded with bowls of comfort that sing with authenticity.

8. Fresh Herbs for Garnish: Don't forget the fresh herbs for garnish! Vietnamese dishes often include a generous handful of cilantro, Thai basil, and mint for added fragrance and flavor. Sprinkle them liberally over your dishes just before serving.

These tips are your compass on your Vietnamese culinary voyage. They're not rules set in stone but rather guiding lights to help you navigate the world of plant-based Vietnamese cuisine. Embrace the flavors, explore the techniques, and let the kitchen become your personal pho stall in the bustling streets of Hanoi. Happy cooking!

Vegan Cơm Rang Dưa Cải (Vegan Bok Choy Fried Rice)
See Page 33

Kitchen Essentials

Alright, my culinary comrades, before we embark on this gastronomic journey through the "Vietnamese Vegan Cookbook," let's talk about the indispensable tools that will be your trusty allies in the kitchen. Vietnamese cuisine is a world of flavors, and having the right equipment at your disposal makes all the difference.

1. Chef's Knife: First and foremost, a good-quality chef's knife is your kitchen workhorse. It'll be your partner in chopping, dicing, and slicing everything from herbs to tofu. Keep it sharp, and it will serve you well.

2. Cutting Board: A sturdy cutting board is essential to protect your countertops and keep your knife in good shape. Look for one that's easy to clean and won't dull your knife's edge.

3. Mortar and Pestle: A mortar and pestle are invaluable for grinding spices and herbs. It's the secret to releasing the aromatic oils and flavors that are the heart of many Vietnamese dishes.

4. Wok or Stir-Fry Pan: For those sizzling stir-fries and quick sautés, a wok or stir-fry pan is a must. Its high sides and even heat distribution make it perfect for tossing ingredients to perfection.

5. Rice Cooker: In Vietnamese cuisine, rice is king. A rice cooker ensures fluffy, perfectly cooked rice every time, allowing you to focus on the rest of your meal.

6. Bamboo Steamer: For those delightful steamed dumplings and buns, a bamboo steamer is your ticket to authentic Vietnamese dim sum. It imparts a subtle, earthy aroma to your creations.

7. Soup Pot: Vietnamese soups, like pho and bun rieu, require a good soup pot. Look for one with a heavy bottom for even heating.

8. Slotted Spoon and Chopsticks: These simple tools are perfect for serving noodles, picking up delicate herbs, and enjoying a bowl of pho the traditional way.

9. Microplane Grater: For zesting citrus fruits and grating fresh ginger and garlic, a microplane grater is a small but mighty addition to your kitchen arsenal.

10. Collapsible Steamer Basket: If you're looking to steam veggies or buns without a bamboo steamer, a collapsible steamer basket can be a handy alternative.

Now that you've met your kitchen essentials, let's dive into tips on how to use these tools effectively. Remember, the heart of Vietnamese cooking lies not just in the ingredients but in the techniques, and with the right tools and know-how, you're ready to create authentic Vietnamese breakfasts, lunches, and dinners that will transport your taste buds to the streets of Hanoi or the bustling markets of Saigon. So, sharpen your knives, prep your workstations, and let's embark on this culinary adventure together.

Vegan Tofu Bún Bò Huế (Spicy Noodle Soup)
See Page 19

Flavor Pairing Suggestions

Welcome, my culinary comrades, to the tantalizing world of the "Vietnamese Vegan Cookbook." As we journey through the fragrant and flavorful landscape of plant-based Vietnamese cuisine, let's take a moment to explore the art of flavor pairing. Vietnamese cooking is a symphony of tastes and textures, and understanding the harmony of flavors is your key to creating culinary masterpieces and crafting your own Vietnamese-inspired creations.

1. Lemongrass and Chili Heat: Lemongrass, with its bright, citrusy notes, dances harmoniously with the fiery kick of chilies. Whether you're crafting a lemongrass tofu stir-fry or a spicy lemongrass-infused pho broth, this pairing electrifies your dishes.

2. Mint and Lime Zest: The cooling, fresh notes of mint complement the zesty brightness of lime zest beautifully. Sprinkle fresh mint leaves and lime zest over your noodle salads or spring rolls for a burst of refreshing flavor.

3. Coconut and Basil: Creamy coconut milk and the fragrant, anise-like sweetness of Thai basil are a match made in culinary heaven. Use them together in curries or soups for a velvety, aromatic experience.

4. Tamarind and Palm Sugar: The tangy punch of tamarind and the rich, caramel sweetness of palm sugar are like yin and yang in Vietnamese cuisine. Combine them in sauces and marinades for a complex and balanced flavor profile.

5. Peanut and Hoisin: The nutty richness of peanuts marries beautifully with the sweet depth of hoisin sauce. Whip up a peanut hoisin dipping sauce for your fresh spring rolls or use it as a glaze for tofu and veggies.

6. Ginger and Star Anise: The fiery warmth of ginger and the subtle, licorice-like nuances of star anise create a compelling duo. Add them to your broths and braises for a depth of flavor that's both comforting and complex.

7. Rice Vinegar and Soy Sauce: The gentle acidity of rice vinegar pairs seamlessly with the salty umami of soy sauce. Combine them in dressings and marinades for a well-balanced, savory-sour profile.

8. Cilantro and Scallions: The bright, citrusy notes of cilantro and the mild oniony bite of scallions make a dynamic duo. Use them as garnishes to add freshness and texture to your dishes.

Remember, these pairing suggestions are your passport to Vietnamese flavor exploration. They're not strict rules but rather guiding stars to help you navigate the rich and diverse world of Vietnamese vegan cuisine. Embrace the flavors, savor the moments, and let the kitchen become your personal Vietnamese bistro. Chúc ngon miệng! (Bon appétit!)

INDEX

Chapter 1:
Breakfast Delights

4 servings

180 calories

40 minutes

Vegan Rice Porridge (Cháo Gà Chay)

A comforting Vietnamese classic, this vegan rice porridge is a heartwarming breakfast filled with tradition and flavor.

Ingredients:

- 1 cup jasmine rice
- 8 cups vegetable broth
- 1 cup sliced mushrooms
- 1 cup diced tofu
- 1/2 cup chopped scallions
- 2 cloves garlic, minced
- 1 thumb-sized piece of ginger, sliced
- Salt and pepper to taste
- Soy sauce for serving
- Fresh cilantro for garnish (optional)

Substitutions

- Use brown rice for a healthier option
- Customize with your favorite vegetables
- Add a dash of sesame oil for extra flavor

Directions

1. Rinse the jasmine rice until the water runs clear.
2. In a large pot, bring the vegetable broth to a boil.
3. Add the rice, mushrooms, tofu, scallions, garlic, and ginger.
4. Reduce the heat to a simmer and cook for 30-35 minutes, stirring occasionally, until the rice is soft and creamy.
5. Season with salt and pepper to taste.
6. Serve hot with soy sauce and garnish with fresh cilantro if desired.
7. Enjoy this vegan rice porridge as a nourishing breakfast!

2 servings

320 calories

20 minutes

Vegan Bánh Mì Breakfast Sandwich

Elevate your breakfast with this vegan Bánh Mì sandwich, a fusion of Vietnamese and French flavors that's as delicious as it is unique.

Ingredients:

For the Tofu Marinade:
- 8 oz firm tofu, sliced
- 2 tbsp soy sauce
- 1 tbsp hoisin sauce
- 1 tbsp rice vinegar
- 1 tsp sesame oil

For the Sandwich:
- 1 baguette or French bread, split and toasted
- Vegan mayonnaise
- Sliced cucumbers
- Pickled carrots and daikon (store-bought or homemade)
- Fresh cilantro sprigs
- Sliced jalapeños (optional)
- Salt and pepper to taste

Substitutions

- Add Sriracha sauce for extra heat
- Substitute pickled carrots and daikon with other pickled vegetables
- Use a different bread of your choice

Directions

For the Tofu Marinade:
1. In a bowl, whisk together soy sauce, hoisin sauce, rice vinegar, and sesame oil.
2. Marinate tofu slices in the mixture for at least 15 minutes.
3. Pan-fry tofu in a lightly oiled skillet until golden brown on both sides.
4. Assemble the Sandwich:
5. Spread vegan mayonnaise on toasted baguette halves.
6. Layer tofu slices, sliced cucumbers, pickled carrots and daikon, fresh cilantro, and sliced jalapeños if desired.
7. Season with salt and pepper.
8. Close the sandwich and enjoy your vegan Bánh Mì breakfast!

2 servings

220 calories

25 minutes

Vegan Tofu Scramble with Vegetables

Start your day with a protein-packed vegan tofu scramble, loaded with colorful vegetables and savory seasonings.

Ingredients:

- 8 oz firm tofu, crumbled
- 1/2 red bell pepper, diced
- 1/2 green bell pepper, diced
- 1/2 onion, diced
- 1/2 cup cherry tomatoes, halved
- 2 cloves garlic, minced
- 1/2 tsp turmeric
- 1/2 tsp cumin
- Salt and pepper to taste
- Fresh parsley for garnish (optional)

Substitutions

- Customize with your favorite veggies
- Add vegan cheese or nutritional yeast for extra flavor
- Top with avocado slices

Directions

1. In a skillet, sauté diced onion and garlic until they turn translucent.
2. Add diced red and green bell peppers, and cherry tomatoes.
3. Cook until the vegetables are tender.
4. Push the vegetables to one side of the skillet and add crumbled tofu to the other side.
5. Season tofu with turmeric, cumin, salt, and pepper.
6. Cook and stir until tofu is heated through and lightly browned.
7. Mix tofu with the sautéed vegetables.
8. Garnish with fresh parsley if desired.
9. Serve hot and enjoy this vegan tofu scramble with vegetables!

4 servings

280 calories

45 minutes

Vegan Sticky Rice with Coconut Milk (Xôi Nước Dừa)

Indulge in the rich flavors of coconut milk and sticky rice, a beloved Vietnamese breakfast treat that's both sweet and satisfying.

Ingredients:

- 2 cups glutinous rice
- 1 can (13.5 oz) coconut milk
- 1/2 cup granulated sugar
- 1/4 tsp salt
- Toasted sesame seeds for garnish (optional)

Substitutions

- Drizzle with a bit of coconut cream for extra richness
- Top with fresh fruit like mango or banana slices
- Sprinkle with crushed peanuts for added crunch

Directions

1. Rinse glutinous rice until the water runs clear and soak it in water for 30 minutes.
2. Drain the rice and steam it for about 20-25 minutes until it's soft and sticky.
3. In a separate saucepan, heat coconut milk over low heat.
4. Stir in granulated sugar and salt until dissolved.
5. Pour the sweet coconut milk mixture over the steamed sticky rice.
6. Mix well until the rice is evenly coated and sticky.
7. Serve hot, garnished with toasted sesame seeds if desired.
8. Enjoy this vegan sticky rice with coconut milk for a sweet morning delight!

4 servings

240 calories

30 minutes

Vegan Rice Noodle Soup (Bún Riêu Chay)

Dive into a bowl of comforting vegan rice noodle soup, a Vietnamese favorite known for its flavorful broth and satisfying noodles.

Ingredients:

For the Broth:
- 8 cups vegetable broth
- 1 onion, halved
- 2 cloves garlic, minced
- 1 thumb-sized piece of ginger, sliced
- 1/2 cup tomato paste
- 1/4 cup tamarind paste
- 1/4 cup sugar
- 1/4 cup soy sauce
- Salt and pepper to taste

For the Tofu Patties:
- 8 oz firm tofu
- 1/4 cup diced mushrooms
- 1/4 cup diced shallots
- 1/4 cup diced green onions
- 1 tbsp soy sauce
- 1 tbsp vegetable oil
- 1/2 tsp black salt (kala namak) for eggy flavor (optional)

For Serving:
- Rice noodles, cooked
- Fresh herbs (mint, cilantro)
- Bean sprouts
- Lime wedges
- Chili sauce (optional)

Substitutions

- Use store-bought vegetable broth for convenience
- Adjust sugar and tamarind paste to taste
- Customize toppings with your favorite herbs and vegetables

Directions

For the Broth:
1. In a large pot, combine vegetable broth, onion, garlic, ginger, tomato paste, tamarind paste, sugar, and soy sauce.
2. Season with salt and pepper to taste.
3. Bring to a simmer and let it cook for about 20-25 minutes.
4. Strain the broth and discard solids.

For the Tofu Patties:
5. In a bowl, mash tofu and mix with diced mushrooms, shallots, green onions, soy sauce, vegetable oil, and black salt if using.
6. Form small patties and pan-fry until golden brown on both sides.
7. Assembly:
8. Divide cooked rice noodles among serving bowls.
9. Top with tofu patties, fresh herbs, bean sprouts, and lime wedges.
10. Ladle hot broth over the noodles.
11. Serve with chili sauce if desired.
12. Enjoy your vegan rice noodle soup!

4 servings

160 calories

45 minutes

Vegan Bánh Cuốn (Steamed Rice Rolls)

Ingredients:

For the Rice Rolls:
- 1 cup rice flour
- 2 cups water
- 1/4 cup tapioca flour
- 1/4 tsp turmeric powder
- 1/4 tsp salt
- Cooking oil for brushing
- Sautéed mushrooms and shallots (see recipe below)

For the Sautéed Mushrooms and Shallots:
- 1 cup sliced mushrooms
- 1/4 cup diced shallots
- 2 cloves garlic, minced
- 1 tbsp soy sauce
- 1 tsp sugar
- 1/2 tsp black pepper

For the Dipping Sauce:
- 2 tbsp soy sauce
- 1 tbsp rice vinegar
- 1 tsp sugar
- 1 clove garlic, minced
- Chili flakes (optional)

Substitutions

- Customize the filling with other vegetables or tofu
- Use pre-made rice paper sheets for convenience
- Adjust the dipping sauce to your preferred taste

Delicate and delicious, these vegan Bánh Cuốn rice rolls are a Vietnamese specialty filled with mushrooms and served with dipping sauce.

Directions

For the Rice Rolls:
1. In a blender, combine rice flour, water, tapioca flour, turmeric powder, and salt.
2. Blend until smooth.
3. Heat a non-stick skillet over low heat and brush with cooking oil.
4. Pour a thin layer of the rice flour mixture onto the skillet, swirling to coat the bottom evenly.
5. Cover and cook until the rice sheet sets (about 1-2 minutes).
6. Carefully remove the rice sheet and place it on a clean surface.
7. Repeat with the remaining batter.
8. Fill each rice sheet with sautéed mushrooms and shallots.
9. Roll them up and set aside.

For the Sautéed Mushrooms and Shallots:
10. In a skillet, sauté mushrooms and shallots in oil until softened.
11. Add garlic, soy sauce, sugar, and black pepper. Cook for another minute.

For the Dipping Sauce:
12. Mix soy sauce, rice vinegar, sugar, minced garlic, and chili flakes if using.
13. Serve the Bánh Cuốn with dipping sauce.
14. Enjoy these vegan steamed rice rolls!

4 servings

220 calories

35 minutes

Vegan Rice Flour Crepes (Bánh Xèo)

Crispy on the outside and filled with a savory vegan filling, Bánh Xèo rice flour crepes are a Vietnamese delight that's perfect for breakfast.

Ingredients:

For the Crepe Batter:
- 1 cup rice flour
- 1/4 cup coconut milk
- 1 1/4 cups water
- 1/4 tsp turmeric powder
- 1/2 tsp salt
- Sliced scallions for garnish (optional)

For the Filling:
- 1 cup bean sprouts
- 1/2 cup diced tofu
- 1/4 cup sliced mushrooms
- 1/4 cup sliced bell peppers
- 1/4 cup sliced onions
- Cooking oil for frying
- Vegan fish sauce or soy sauce for dipping

Substitutions

- Add sliced vegan sausage or tempeh for extra protein
- Customize the filling with your favorite vegetables
- Use lettuce leaves as wrappers for a low-carb option

Directions

For the Crepe Batter:
1. In a blender, combine rice flour, coconut milk, water, turmeric powder, and salt.
2. Blend until smooth and let the batter rest for 30 minutes.
3. For the Filling:
4. In a pan, sauté diced tofu, sliced mushrooms, bell peppers, and onions in oil until tender.
5. Assembly:
6. Heat a non-stick skillet over medium-high heat and add oil.
7. Pour a ladle of crepe batter into the skillet, swirling to coat the bottom.
8. Add a portion of the sautéed filling and bean sprouts to one half of the crepe.
9. Cover and cook until the crepe is crispy and golden.
10. Fold the other half of the crepe over the filling.
11. Slide onto a plate, garnish with sliced scallions, and serve hot with vegan fish sauce or soy sauce for dipping.
12. Enjoy these vegan Bánh Xèo rice flour crepes!

4 servings | 280 calories | 20 minutes

Vegan Breakfast Fried Rice

Turn leftover rice into a flavorful breakfast with this vegan fried rice recipe, packed with veggies and Asian-inspired seasonings.

Ingredients:

- 3 cups cooked jasmine rice, cold
- 1/2 cup diced tofu
- 1/2 cup frozen peas and carrots
- 1/2 cup diced bell peppers
- 1/2 cup chopped scallions
- 2 cloves garlic, minced
- 2 tbsp soy sauce
- 1 tbsp sesame oil
- 1/2 tsp turmeric powder
- Salt and pepper to taste
- Cooking oil for frying

Substitutions

- Customize with your favorite vegetables or leftover cooked veggies
- Add a dash of Sriracha for extra heat
- Top with sesame seeds for garnish

Directions

1. Heat cooking oil in a large skillet over medium-high heat.
2. Add minced garlic and sauté until fragrant.
3. Add diced tofu and cook until it starts to brown.
4. Stir in frozen peas and carrots, diced bell peppers, and chopped scallions.
5. Cook until the vegetables are tender.
6. Add cold cooked jasmine rice to the skillet.
7. Drizzle with soy sauce, sesame oil, and sprinkle turmeric powder over the rice.
8. Stir-fry until everything is well combined and heated through.
9. Season with salt and pepper to taste.
10. Serve hot as a delightful vegan breakfast fried rice!

2 servings

300 calories

15 minutes

Vegan Bánh Mì Omelette

Experience the flavors of a classic Bánh Mì in omelette form with this vegan breakfast delight, perfect for a quick and satisfying meal.

Ingredients:

- 1 cup chickpea flour
- 1 cup water
- 1/4 cup sliced scallions
- 1/4 cup sliced bell peppers
- 1/4 cup shredded carrots
- 1/4 cup chopped cilantro
- 1/4 cup sliced cucumbers
- Vegan mayonnaise
- Vegan pâté (optional)
- Sliced jalapeños (optional)
- Cooking oil for frying
- Salt and pepper to taste

Substitutions

- Add vegan cheese for extra richness
- Customize with your favorite Bánh Mì ingredients
- Use whole chickpeas or other legume flours as a substitute

Directions

1. In a bowl, whisk chickpea flour and water until smooth.
2. Stir in sliced scallions, bell peppers, shredded carrots, and chopped cilantro.
3. Heat cooking oil in a non-stick skillet over medium heat.
4. Pour half of the chickpea flour mixture into the skillet.
5. Cook until the edges start to set.
6. Carefully flip the omelette and cook the other side until golden brown.
7. Repeat with the remaining mixture to make another omelette.
8. Assembly:
9. Spread vegan mayonnaise and vegan pâté (if using) on one side of each omelette.
10. Top with sliced cucumbers and jalapeños if desired.
11. Season with salt and pepper to taste.
12. Fold the omelettes and serve hot as vegan Bánh Mì omelettes!
13. Enjoy the fusion of flavors!

4 servings

220 calories

35 minutes

Vegan Vietnamese-Style Pancakes (Bánh Khọt)

These mini Vietnamese-style pancakes, known as Bánh Khot, are a delightful breakfast treat filled with savory flavors and crispy edges.

Ingredients:

- 1 cup rice flour
- 1/4 cup coconut milk
- 1 cup water
- 1/4 tsp turmeric powder
- 1/4 tsp salt
- 1/4 cup diced tofu
- 1/4 cup diced mushrooms
- 1/4 cup diced scallions
- Cooking oil for frying
- Vegan fish sauce or soy sauce for dipping

Substitutions

- Customize the filling with your favorite veggies or protein
- Top with fresh herbs for extra freshness
- Use a regular non-stick skillet if you don't have a Bánh Khot pan

Directions

1. In a blender, combine rice flour, coconut milk, water, turmeric powder, and salt.
2. Blend until smooth and let the batter rest for 30 minutes.
3. In a separate bowl, mix diced tofu, diced mushrooms, and diced scallions.
4. Heat a Bánh Khot pan or a small non-stick skillet over medium-high heat and add a drop of cooking oil to each mold.
5. Pour a small amount of the batter into each mold, followed by the tofu-mushroom-scallion mixture.
6. Cover and cook until the edges are crispy and golden.
7. Carefully remove the mini pancakes from the molds.
8. Serve hot with vegan fish sauce or soy sauce for dipping.
9. Enjoy these vegan Bánh Khot Vietnamese-style pancakes!

Chapter 2:
Lunch Classics

4 servings

240 calories

45 minutes

Vegan Phở Chay (Vietnamese Noodle Soup)

A vegan twist on the iconic Vietnamese Phở, this hearty noodle soup is brimming with aromatic herbs and spices, making it a satisfying lunchtime classic.

Ingredients:

For the Broth:
- 8 cups vegetable broth
- 1 onion, halved
- 2 cloves garlic, minced
- 1 thumb-sized piece of ginger, sliced
- 2 cinnamon sticks
- 4 star anise pods
- 4 cloves
- 1/4 cup soy sauce
- 1 tbsp agave syrup (or sweetener of choice)
- Salt and pepper to taste

For Serving:
- Rice noodles, cooked
- Sliced tofu (pre-fried or pan-fried)
- Bean sprouts
- Fresh herbs (cilantro, Thai basil, mint)
- Lime wedges
- Sliced chili peppers (optional)

Substitutions

- Customize toppings with your favorite vegetables
- Use vegetable-based protein alternatives
- Adjust the spice level to your preference

Directions

For the Broth:
1. In a large pot, combine vegetable broth, onion, garlic, ginger, cinnamon sticks, star anise, cloves, soy sauce, and agave syrup.
2. Season with salt and pepper to taste.
3. Bring to a simmer and let it cook for about 30 minutes.
4. Strain the broth and discard solids.

Assembly:
5. Divide cooked rice noodles among serving bowls.
6. Add sliced tofu and bean sprouts.
7. Ladle hot broth over the noodles and tofu.
8. Serve with fresh herbs, lime wedges, and sliced chili peppers if desired.
9. Enjoy your vegan Phở Chay!

4 servings

220 calories

30 minutes

Vegan Bún Chay (Vietnamese Noodle Salad)

Experience the vibrant flavors of Vietnam with this vegan Bún Chay noodle salad, a colorful medley of fresh herbs, veggies, and vermicelli noodles.

Ingredients:

For the Salad:
- 8 oz vermicelli rice noodles, cooked
- Lettuce leaves
- Cucumber slices
- Bean sprouts
- Fresh herbs (mint, cilantro, Thai basil)
- Crushed peanuts
- Lime wedges
- Sliced chili peppers (optional)

For the Dressing:
- 1/4 cup soy sauce
- 2 tbsp rice vinegar
- 2 tbsp agave syrup (or sweetener of choice)
- 2 cloves garlic, minced
- 1 tsp sriracha sauce (adjust to taste)

Directions

For the Salad:
1. Arrange lettuce leaves, cucumber slices, bean sprouts, and fresh herbs on serving plates.
2. Top with cooked vermicelli rice noodles.
3. Sprinkle crushed peanuts over the noodles.
4. Garnish with lime wedges and sliced chili peppers if desired.

For the Dressing:
5. In a small bowl, whisk together soy sauce, rice vinegar, agave syrup, minced garlic, and sriracha sauce.
6. Drizzle the dressing over the salad.
7. Toss to combine and enjoy your vegan Bún Chay noodle salad!

Substitutions

- Add your choice of protein (tofu, tempeh, seitan)
- Customize with your favorite vegetables
- Adjust the dressing to your preferred taste

4 servings

280 calories

40 minutes

Vegan Cơm Gà Chay (Vegan "Chicken" Rice)

Savor the flavors of Vietnam with this vegan twist on Cơm Gà, featuring tender "chicken"-style soy protein served over fragrant rice and a side of zesty dipping sauce.

Ingredients:

For the "Chicken" Marinade:
- 8 oz vegan "chicken" (seitan or soy-based), sliced
- 2 cloves garlic, minced
- 1 thumb-sized piece of ginger, minced
- 2 tbsp soy sauce
- 1 tbsp vegetable oil
- 1 tsp sugar

For the Dipping Sauce:
- 2 tbsp soy sauce
- 1 tbsp lime juice
- 1 tbsp agave syrup (or sweetener of choice)
- 1 clove garlic, minced
- Sliced chili peppers (optional)

Substitutions

- Use your favorite vegan protein (tofu, tempeh)
- Customize the dipping sauce with your preferred level of spiciness
- Add fresh herbs for garnish

Directions

For the "Chicken" Marinade:
1. In a bowl, combine minced garlic, minced ginger, soy sauce, vegetable oil, and sugar.
2. Add sliced vegan "chicken" and marinate for at least 15 minutes.
3. Heat a pan over medium-high heat and pan-fry the marinated "chicken" until golden brown and cooked through.

For the Dipping Sauce:
4. In a small bowl, mix soy sauce, lime juice, agave syrup, minced garlic, and sliced chili peppers if desired.
5. Serve the "chicken" over cooked rice with the dipping sauce on the side.
6. Enjoy your vegan Cơm Gà Chay!

4 servings | 300 calories | 30 minutes

Vegan Cơm Tấm (Broken Rice)

Dive into the Vietnamese culinary world with Cơm Tấm, a delicious dish featuring broken rice, grilled "pork," and a side of zesty sauce.

Ingredients:

For the Grilled "Pork":
- 8 oz vegan "pork" (seitan or soy-based), sliced
- 2 cloves garlic, minced
- 1 thumb-sized piece of ginger, minced
- 2 tbsp soy sauce
- 1 tbsp vegetable oil
- 1 tsp sugar

For the Dipping Sauce:
- 2 tbsp soy sauce
- 1 tbsp lime juice
- 1 tbsp agave syrup (or sweetener of choice)
- 1 clove garlic, minced
- Sliced chili peppers (optional)

For Serving:
- Broken rice (Cơm Tấm)
- Fresh vegetables (sliced cucumber, lettuce, tomato)
- Pickled vegetables (optional)

Substitutions

- Customize the dish with your preferred vegetables
- Add crushed peanuts for extra crunch
- Adjust the dipping sauce to your taste

Directions

For the Grilled "Pork":
1. In a bowl, combine minced garlic, minced ginger, soy sauce, vegetable oil, and sugar.
2. Add sliced vegan "pork" and marinate for at least 15 minutes.
3. Heat a grill pan or skillet over medium-high heat and grill the marinated "pork" slices until charred and cooked through.

For the Dipping Sauce:
4. In a small bowl, mix soy sauce, lime juice, agave syrup, minced garlic, and sliced chili peppers if desired.
5. Serve the grilled "pork" over broken rice with fresh vegetables, pickled vegetables (if using), and the dipping sauce on the side.
6. Enjoy your vegan Cơm Tấm!

2 servings

320 calories

20 minutes

Vegan Bánh Mì Chay (Vegan Vietnamese Sandwich)

Indulge in the flavors of Vietnam with this vegan Bánh Mì sandwich, featuring crusty bread filled with marinated tofu, fresh vegetables, and zesty sauce.

Ingredients:

For the Marinated Tofu:
- 8 oz tofu, sliced
- 2 cloves garlic, minced
- 2 tbsp soy sauce
- 1 tbsp vegetable oil
- 1 tsp sugar

For Serving:
- Crusty baguette or bread rolls
- Vegan mayonnaise
- Sliced cucumber
- Pickled daikon and carrots (Đồ Chua)
- Fresh cilantro leaves
- Sliced jalapeños (optional)

Substitutions

- Customize with your favorite Bánh Mì toppings
- Use other protein alternatives like tempeh or seitan
- Adjust the spice level with more jalapeños

Directions

For the Marinated Tofu:
1. In a bowl, combine minced garlic, soy sauce, vegetable oil, and sugar.
2. Add sliced tofu and marinate for at least 15 minutes.
3. Heat a pan over medium-high heat and pan-fry the marinated tofu slices until golden brown.

Assembly:
4. Slice the baguette or bread rolls in half.
5. Spread vegan mayonnaise on both sides of the bread.
6. Layer with sliced cucumber, pickled daikon and carrots (Đồ Chua), marinated tofu, fresh cilantro leaves, and sliced jalapeños if desired.
7. Press the sandwich together and serve.
8. Enjoy your vegan Bánh Mì Chay!

4 servings

180 calories

30 minutes

Vegan Gỏi Cuốn (Fresh Spring Rolls)

Dive into the world of Vietnamese cuisine with these vegan Gỏi Cuốn fresh spring rolls, featuring translucent rice paper filled with fresh herbs, tofu, and dipping sauce.

Ingredients:

For the Spring Rolls:
- Rice paper sheets
- Lettuce leaves
- Fresh herbs (mint, cilantro, Thai basil)
- Thin rice vermicelli noodles, cooked
- Sliced tofu (pre-fried or pan-fried)
- Bean sprouts
- Sliced cucumber
- Sliced carrot
- Rice paper sheets

For the Dipping Sauce:
- 2 tbsp hoisin sauce
- 2 tbsp peanut butter
- 1 tbsp soy sauce
- 1 clove garlic, minced
- Water (to adjust consistency)
- Crushed peanuts (for garnish)

Substitutions

- Customize the fillings with your favorite vegetables and herbs
- Use your preferred dipping sauce
- Add sliced avocado for creaminess

Directions

For the Spring Rolls:
1. Prepare a shallow dish of warm water.
2. Dip one rice paper sheet into the water until it softens (about 15 seconds).
3. Place the softened rice paper on a clean surface.
4. Layer with lettuce leaves, fresh herbs, cooked vermicelli noodles, sliced tofu, bean sprouts, sliced cucumber, and sliced carrot.
5. Fold the sides of the rice paper over the fillings and roll up tightly.
6. Repeat with the remaining ingredients.

For the Dipping Sauce:
7. In a bowl, whisk together hoisin sauce, peanut butter, soy sauce, minced garlic, and a little water to achieve the desired consistency.
8. Sprinkle crushed peanuts over the sauce for garnish.
9. Serve the spring rolls with the dipping sauce.
10. Enjoy your vegan Gỏi Cuốn fresh spring rolls!

4 servings • 260 calories • 50 minutes

Vegan Tofu Bún Bò Huế (Spicy Noodle Soup)

Spice up your lunchtime with this vegan Tofu Bún Bò Huế, a flavorful Vietnamese noodle soup that's both aromatic and satisfying.

Ingredients:

For the Broth:
- 8 cups vegetable broth
- 1 onion, halved
- 2 cloves garlic, minced
- 1 thumb-sized piece of ginger, sliced
- 2 lemongrass stalks, smashed
- 2 tbsp soy sauce
- 1 tbsp vegetable oil
- 1 tsp sugar
- Salt and pepper to taste

For Serving:
- Rice vermicelli noodles, cooked
- Sliced tofu (pre-fried or pan-fried)
- Fresh herbs (cilantro, Thai basil, mint)
- Lime wedges
- Sliced chili peppers (optional)

Substitutions

- Customize the spice level with more chili peppers
- Add sliced mushrooms or other vegetables
- Adjust the herbs to your preference

Directions

For the Broth:
1. In a large pot, combine vegetable broth, onion, garlic, ginger, lemongrass, soy sauce, vegetable oil, and sugar.
2. Season with salt and pepper to taste.
3. Bring to a simmer and let it cook for about 40 minutes.
4. Strain the broth and discard solids.

Assembly:
5. Divide cooked rice vermicelli noodles among serving bowls.
6. Add sliced tofu and fresh herbs.
7. Ladle hot broth over the noodles and tofu.
8. Serve with lime wedges and sliced chili peppers if desired.
9. Enjoy your vegan Tofu Bún Bò Huế!

4 servings

280 calories

50 minutes

Vegan Cá Kho Tộ (Braised Tofu in Clay Pot)

Immerse yourself in the rich flavors of Vietnam with this vegan Cá Kho Tộ, featuring tender braised tofu in a savory caramel sauce, served with steamed rice.

Ingredients:

For the Braised Tofu:
- 8 oz firm tofu, cubed
- 2 cloves garlic, minced
- 1 thumb-sized piece of ginger, sliced
- 2 tbsp soy sauce
- 1 tbsp vegetable oil
- 1 tsp sugar
- 1/4 cup water

For Serving:
- Steamed rice
- Fresh cilantro leaves
- Sliced green onions
- Sliced chili peppers (optional)

Substitutions

- Customize with your favorite vegetables
- Adjust the sauce sweetness to your taste
- Use other protein alternatives like seitan or tempeh

Directions

For the Braised Tofu:
1. In a clay pot or skillet, heat vegetable oil over medium heat.
2. Add minced garlic and sliced ginger, sauté until fragrant.
3. Add cubed tofu and pan-fry until golden brown on all sides.
4. Stir in soy sauce and sugar, allowing it to caramelize.
5. Pour in water and simmer until the sauce thickens and coats the tofu.

Assembly:
6. Serve the braised tofu over steamed rice.
7. Garnish with fresh cilantro leaves, sliced green onions, and sliced chili peppers if desired.
8. Enjoy your vegan Cá Kho Tộ!

4 servings

260 calories

25 minutes

Vegan Cơm Chiên Chay (Vegan Fried Rice)

Elevate your lunchtime with this vegan Cơm Chiên Chay fried rice, a delightful mix of aromatic flavors and colorful vegetables that's quick to prepare.

Ingredients:

For the Fried Rice:
- Cooked jasmine rice, cold
- 2 cloves garlic, minced
- 1/4 cup frozen peas and carrots
- 1/4 cup diced bell peppers
- 2 scallions, chopped
- 2 tbsp soy sauce
- 1 tsp sesame oil
- 1/4 tsp turmeric powder (for color)
- Salt and pepper to taste
- Cooking oil for frying

Substitutions

- Customize with your favorite vegetables or leftover cooked veggies
- Add a dash of Sriracha for extra heat
- Top with sesame seeds for garnish

Directions

For the Fried Rice:
1. Heat cooking oil in a large skillet over medium-high heat.
2. Add minced garlic and sauté until fragrant.
3. Add frozen peas and carrots, diced bell peppers, and chopped scallions.
4. Cook until the vegetables are tender.
5. Add cold cooked jasmine rice to the skillet.
6. Drizzle with soy sauce, sesame oil, and sprinkle turmeric powder over the rice.
7. Stir-fry until everything is well combined and heated through.
8. Season with salt and pepper to taste.
9. Serve hot as a delightful vegan breakfast fried rice!

4 servings

240 calories

40 minutes

Vegan Bún Riêu Chay (Vegan Crab Noodle Soup)

Ingredients:

For the "Crab" Cakes:
- 8 oz firm tofu, mashed
- 1/4 cup wood ear mushrooms, finely chopped
- 2 cloves garlic, minced
- 2 scallions, chopped
- 2 tsp soy sauce
- 1 tsp sugar
- 1/4 tsp black salt (kala namak, for an eggy flavor)
- Vegetable oil for pan-frying

For the Broth:
- 8 cups vegetable broth
- 1 cup canned crushed tomatoes
- 1 thumb-sized piece of tamarind pulp
- 1 tbsp vegetable oil
- 1 onion, chopped
- 2 cloves garlic, minced
- 1 thumb-sized piece of ginger, minced
- 2 tbsp soy sauce
- 1 tbsp agave syrup (or sweetener of choice)
- Salt and pepper to taste

For Serving:
- Rice vermicelli noodles, cooked
- Fresh herbs (cilantro, Thai basil, mint)
- Bean sprouts
- Lime wedges
- Sliced chili peppers (optional)

Substitutions
- Customize the spice level with more chili peppers
- Add fresh pineapple chunks for sweetness
- Adjust the tamarind for sourness

Enjoy the flavors of Vietnam with this vegan Bún Riêu Chay noodle soup, featuring tofu "crab" cakes in a savory tomato-based broth.

Directions

For the "Crab" Cakes:
1. In a bowl, combine mashed tofu, chopped wood ear mushrooms, minced garlic, chopped scallions, soy sauce, sugar, and black salt.
2. Form the mixture into small "crab" cakes.
3. Heat vegetable oil in a pan over medium-high heat and pan-fry the "crab" cakes until golden brown on both sides.

For the Broth:
4. In a large pot, heat vegetable oil over medium heat.
5. Add chopped onion, minced garlic, and minced ginger, sauté until fragrant.
6. Add vegetable broth, crushed tomatoes, tamarind pulp, soy sauce, agave syrup, salt, and pepper.
7. Simmer for about 30 minutes, then strain the broth to remove solids.

Assembly:
8. Divide cooked rice vermicelli noodles among serving bowls.
9. Add bean sprouts and fresh herbs.
10. Place the pan-fried "crab" cakes on top.
11. Ladle hot broth over the noodles and "crab" cakes.
12. Serve with lime wedges and sliced chili peppers if desired.
13. Enjoy your vegan Bún Riêu Chay!

Chapter 3:
Dinner Sensations

4 servings

290 calories

50 minutes

Vegan Cà Ri Chay (Vietnamese Curry)

Normal

Experience the heartwarming flavors of Vietnamese Cà Ri Chay, a delectable curry filled with colorful vegetables and tofu, served with steamed rice.

Ingredients:

For the Curry Paste:
- 2 cloves garlic, minced
- 1 thumb-sized piece of ginger, minced
- 1 lemongrass stalk, minced
- 1 red chili pepper, minced (adjust to spice preference)
- 1 tsp curry powder
- 1 tsp turmeric powder
- 1/4 cup vegetable broth

For the Curry:
- 2 cups mixed vegetables (potatoes, carrots, bell peppers)
- 1 cup tofu, cubed
- 1 can coconut milk
- 2 cups vegetable broth
- 1 tbsp soy sauce
- 1 tbsp agave syrup (or sweetener of choice)
- Salt and pepper to taste
- Cooking oil for sautéing

Substitutions

- Customize the vegetables to your preference
- Adjust the spiciness with more or fewer chili peppers
- Use tempeh or seitan instead of tofu

Directions

For the Curry Paste:
1. In a blender, combine minced garlic, minced ginger, minced lemongrass, minced red chili pepper, curry powder, turmeric powder, and vegetable broth.
2. Blend into a smooth paste.

For the Curry:
3. In a pot, heat cooking oil over medium heat.
4. Add the curry paste and sauté until fragrant.
5. Add mixed vegetables and tofu cubes, stir to coat in the paste.
6. Pour in coconut milk and vegetable broth.
7. Season with soy sauce, agave syrup, salt, and pepper.
8. Simmer until vegetables are tender.
9. Serve with steamed rice and enjoy your vegan Cà Ri Chay!

4 servings

180 calories

30 minutes

Vegan Gỏi Mít Trộn (Jackfruit Salad)

Delight in the fresh flavors of Gỏi Mít Trộn, a Vietnamese jackfruit salad bursting with vibrant herbs, crispy shallots, and a zesty dressing.

Ingredients:

For the Salad:
- 1 can young green jackfruit in brine, drained and shredded
- Fresh herbs (mint, cilantro, Thai basil)
- Sliced cucumber
- Sliced carrot
- Crushed roasted peanuts
- Crispy fried shallots

For the Dressing:
- 2 tbsp lime juice
- 1 tbsp soy sauce
- 1 tbsp agave syrup (or sweetener of choice)
- 1 clove garlic, minced
- Sliced chili peppers (optional)

Directions

For the Salad:
1. In a large bowl, combine shredded jackfruit, fresh herbs, sliced cucumber, sliced carrot, crushed peanuts, and crispy fried shallots.

For the Dressing:
2. In a small bowl, whisk together lime juice, soy sauce, agave syrup, minced garlic, and sliced chili peppers if desired.
3. Drizzle the dressing over the salad and toss to combine.
4. Enjoy your vegan Gỏi Mít Trộn!

Substitutions

- Add more vegetables like bean sprouts or bell peppers
- Adjust the dressing's sweetness and spiciness to your taste
- Garnish with sesame seeds for extra flavor

4 servings

210 calories

40 minutes

Vegan Hủ tiếu Chay (Clear Noodle Soup)

Transport your taste buds to Vietnam with this vegan Hủ tiếu Chay, a clear noodle soup brimming with tofu, mushrooms, and fresh herbs.

Ingredients:

For the Broth:
- 8 cups vegetable broth
- 2 cloves garlic, minced
- 1 thumb-sized piece of ginger, sliced
- 2 star anise pods
- 1 cinnamon stick
- 1/4 cup soy sauce
- 1 tbsp agave syrup (or sweetener of choice)
- Salt and pepper to taste

For Serving:
- Clear rice noodles, cooked
- Sliced tofu (pre-fried or pan-fried)
- Sliced mushrooms (shiitake or oyster mushrooms)
- Fresh herbs (cilantro, Thai basil, mint)
- Lime wedges
- Sliced chili peppers (optional)

Directions

For the Broth:
1. In a large pot, combine vegetable broth, minced garlic, sliced ginger, star anise pods, cinnamon stick, soy sauce, agave syrup, salt, and pepper.
2. Bring to a simmer and let it cook for about 30 minutes.
3. Strain the broth and discard solids.

Assembly:
4. Divide cooked clear rice noodles among serving bowls.
5. Add sliced tofu, sliced mushrooms, and fresh herbs.
6. Ladle hot broth over the noodles and tofu.
7. Serve with lime wedges and sliced chili peppers if desired.
8. Enjoy your vegan Hủ tiếu Chay!

Substitutions

- Customize the soup with your preferred mushrooms
- Adjust the spice level with more chili peppers
- Add bean sprouts for extra freshness

4 servings

260 calories

35 minutes

Vegan Bún Thịt Nướng (Grilled Tofu Noodles)

Savor the flavors of Vietnam with this vegan Bún Thịt Nướng, featuring marinated grilled tofu served over vermicelli noodles, fresh herbs, and a zesty sauce.

Ingredients:

For the Marinade:
- 1/4 cup soy sauce
- 2 cloves garlic, minced
- 1 thumb-sized piece of ginger, minced
- 2 tbsp agave syrup (or sweetener of choice)
- 1 tsp sriracha sauce (adjust to spice preference)

For Serving:
- Rice vermicelli noodles, cooked
- Fresh herbs (cilantro, Thai basil, mint)
- Sliced cucumber
- Crushed roasted peanuts
- Lime wedges
- Vegan dipping sauce

Substitutions

- Customize the toppings with your favorite vegetables
- Adjust the marinade's spiciness to your taste
- Use your preferred dipping sauce

Directions

For the Marinade:
1. In a bowl, whisk together soy sauce, minced garlic, minced ginger, agave syrup, and sriracha sauce.
2. Marinate tofu slices in the mixture for at least 15 minutes.
3. Grill or pan-fry the tofu until nicely charred.

Assembly:
4. Divide cooked rice vermicelli noodles among serving bowls.
5. Top with grilled tofu, fresh herbs, sliced cucumber, crushed peanuts, and lime wedges.
6. Serve with vegan dipping sauce on the side.
7. Enjoy your vegan Bún Thịt Nướng!

4 servings · 160 calories · 30 minutes

Vegan Canh Chua Chay (Sour Soup)

Brighten your dinner table with this vegan Canh Chua Chay, a tangy and savory Vietnamese sour soup loaded with vegetables and tofu.

Ingredients:

For the Soup:
- 8 cups vegetable broth
- 1 thumb-sized piece of tamarind pulp
- 1/4 cup soy sauce
- 2 tbsp agave syrup (or sweetener of choice)
- 1/2 cup sliced tomatoes
- 1/2 cup sliced okra
- 1/2 cup sliced pineapple
- 1/2 cup sliced bean sprouts
- 1 cup sliced tofu (pre-fried or pan-fried)
- Sliced chili peppers (optional)
- Fresh herbs (cilantro, Thai basil, mint)
- Lime wedges

Substitutions

- Customize the soup with your preferred vegetables
- Adjust the tamarind for sourness
- Add more chili peppers for extra spice

Directions

For the Soup:
1. In a large pot, combine vegetable broth, tamarind pulp, soy sauce, agave syrup, sliced tomatoes, sliced okra, and sliced pineapple.
2. Bring to a boil and simmer for about 10 minutes until vegetables are tender.
3. Strain the tamarind pulp and discard solids.
4. Add sliced bean sprouts and tofu to the soup.
5. Season with sliced chili peppers if desired.
6. Serve hot with fresh herbs and lime wedges.
7. Enjoy your vegan Canh Chua Chay!

4 servings

220 calories

30 minutes

Vegan Lemongrass Tofu Stir-Fry

Elevate your dinner with this vegan Lemongrass Tofu Stir-Fry, a fragrant and flavorful dish that combines tofu, lemongrass, and fresh vegetables.

Ingredients:

For the Stir-Fry:
- 1 cup sliced tofu (pre-fried or pan-fried)
- 2 cloves garlic, minced
- 1 thumb-sized piece of lemongrass, minced
- 1 red chili pepper, sliced (adjust to spice preference)
- Sliced bell peppers
- Sliced zucchini
- Sliced carrots
- Sliced snap peas
- Sliced mushrooms (shiitake or oyster mushrooms)
- 2 tbsp soy sauce
- 1 tbsp agave syrup (or sweetener of choice)
- Cooking oil for stir-frying

Substitutions

- Customize the stir-fry with your favorite vegetables
- Adjust the spiciness with more or fewer chili peppers
- Add cashews or peanuts for extra crunch

Directions

For the Stir-Fry:
1. Heat cooking oil in a wok or large skillet over high heat.
2. Add minced garlic, minced lemongrass, and sliced red chili pepper.
3. Stir-fry for about a minute until fragrant.
4. Add sliced tofu and stir-fry until heated through.
5. Add sliced bell peppers, zucchini, carrots, snap peas, and mushrooms.
6. Continue to stir-fry until vegetables are tender-crisp.
7. Drizzle with soy sauce and agave syrup, tossing to coat evenly.
8. Serve hot and enjoy your vegan Lemongrass Tofu Stir-Fry!

4 servings

240 calories

45 minutes

Vegan Cơm Hến Chay (Vegan Clam Rice)

Dive into the unique flavors of Cơm Hến Chay, a Vietnamese vegan clam rice dish featuring aromatic rice, crispy tofu, and a zesty dressing.

Ingredients:

For the Rice:
- 2 cups cooked jasmine rice
- 1 cup crispy fried tofu
- Fresh herbs (cilantro, Thai basil, mint)
- Sliced cucumber
- Crushed roasted peanuts

For the Dressing:
- 2 tbsp soy sauce
- 1 tbsp agave syrup (or sweetener of choice)
- 1 clove garlic, minced
- Sliced chili peppers (optional)

Directions

For the Rice:
1. In a large bowl, combine cooked jasmine rice, crispy fried tofu, fresh herbs, sliced cucumber, and crushed roasted peanuts.

For the Dressing:
2. In a small bowl, whisk together soy sauce, agave syrup, minced garlic, and sliced chili peppers if desired.
3. Drizzle the dressing over the rice mixture and toss to combine.
4. Enjoy your vegan Cơm Hến Chay!

Substitutions

- Customize with your preferred herbs and vegetables
- Adjust the dressing's sweetness and spiciness to your taste
- Garnish with sesame seeds for extra flavor

4 servings

290 calories

40 minutes

Vegan Mì Quảng (Turmeric Noodles)

Indulge in the vibrant flavors of Mì Quảng, a Vietnamese turmeric noodle dish featuring tofu, fresh herbs, and a flavorful broth.

Ingredients:

For the Broth:
- 8 cups vegetable broth
- 1 thumb-sized piece of ginger, sliced
- 1 thumb-sized piece of turmeric, sliced
- 2 cloves garlic, minced
- 1 lemongrass stalk, smashed
- 2 star anise pods
- 1/4 cup soy sauce
- 1 tbsp agave syrup (or sweetener of choice)
- Salt and pepper to taste

For Serving:
- Thick rice noodles, cooked
- Sliced tofu (pre-fried or pan-fried)
- Fresh herbs (cilantro, Thai basil, mint)
- Bean sprouts
- Lime wedges
- Crushed roasted peanuts

Directions

For the Broth:
1. In a large pot, combine vegetable broth, sliced ginger, sliced turmeric, minced garlic, smashed lemongrass, star anise pods, soy sauce, agave syrup, salt, and pepper.
2. Bring to a boil and simmer for about 20 minutes.
3. Strain the broth and discard solids.

Assembly:
4. Divide cooked thick rice noodles among serving bowls.
5. Top with sliced tofu, fresh herbs, bean sprouts, and a squeeze of lime juice.
6. Ladle hot broth over the noodles and tofu.
7. Garnish with crushed roasted peanuts.
8. Enjoy your vegan Mì Quảng!

Substitutions

- Customize the toppings with your favorite vegetables
- Adjust the spice level with more chili peppers
- Add crispy shallots for extra flavor

4 servings

220 calories

50 minutes

Vegan Bánh Canh Chay (Tapioca Noodle Soup)

Warm your soul with this vegan Bánh Canh Chay, a comforting tapioca noodle soup with a hearty mix of mushrooms and tofu.

Ingredients:

For the Broth:
- 8 cups vegetable broth
- 2 cloves garlic, minced
- 1 thumb-sized piece of ginger, sliced
- 1/4 cup soy sauce
- 1 tbsp agave syrup (or sweetener of choice)
- Salt and pepper to taste

For Serving:
- Tapioca noodles, cooked
- Sliced tofu (pre-fried or pan-fried)
- Sliced mushrooms (shiitake or oyster mushrooms)
- Sliced scallions
- Sliced chili peppers (optional)
- Fresh herbs (cilantro, Thai basil, mint)
- Lime wedges

Substitutions

- Customize the soup with your preferred mushrooms
- Adjust the spice level with more chili peppers
- Add fried shallots for extra flavor

Directions

For the Broth:
1. In a large pot, combine vegetable broth, minced garlic, sliced ginger, soy sauce, agave syrup, salt, and pepper.
2. Bring to a boil and simmer for about 30 minutes.
3. Strain the broth and discard solids.

Assembly:
4. Divide cooked tapioca noodles among serving bowls.
5. Top with sliced tofu, sliced mushrooms, sliced scallions, and sliced chili peppers if desired.
6. Ladle hot broth over the noodles and toppings.
7. Garnish with fresh herbs and lime wedges.
8. Enjoy your vegan Bánh Canh Chay!

4 servings

250 calories

30 minutes

Vegan Cơm Rang Dưa Cải (Vegan Bok Choy Fried Rice)

Enjoy the simplicity of Cơm Rang Dưa Cải, a vegan bok choy fried rice dish that combines the earthy flavors of bok choy with fragrant rice and savory seasonings.

Ingredients:

For the Fried Rice:
- Cooked jasmine rice, cold
- 2 cloves garlic, minced
- 1 thumb-sized piece of ginger, minced
- 1 cup sliced bok choy
- 1/4 cup sliced shiitake mushrooms
- 2 tbsp soy sauce
- 1 tsp sesame oil
- Salt and pepper to taste
- Cooking oil for frying

Substitutions

- Customize with your favorite vegetables or leftover cooked veggies
- Add a dash of Sriracha for extra heat
- Top with sesame seeds for garnish

Directions

For the Fried Rice:
1. Heat cooking oil in a large skillet over medium-high heat.
2. Add minced garlic and minced ginger, sauté until fragrant.
3. Add sliced bok choy and shiitake mushrooms, stir-fry until tender.
4. Add cold cooked jasmine rice to the skillet.
5. Drizzle with soy sauce and sesame oil, sprinkle salt and pepper to taste.
6. Stir-fry until everything is well combined and heated through.
7. Serve hot as a delightful vegan bok choy fried rice!

Chapter 4:
Tofu Temptations

4 servings

240 calories

35 minutes

Vegan Lemongrass Chili Tofu

Spice up your dinner with this Vegan Lemongrass Chili Tofu, where crispy tofu is bathed in a fragrant lemongrass and chili sauce.

Ingredients:

For the Tofu:
- 1 block of extra-firm tofu, cubed and fried

For the Lemongrass Chili Sauce:
- 2 stalks lemongrass, minced
- 3 cloves garlic, minced
- 2 red chili peppers, sliced (adjust to spice preference)
- 2 tbsp soy sauce
- 1 tbsp agave syrup (or sweetener of choice)
- Juice of 1 lime
- Cooking oil for frying

Substitutions

- Adjust the spiciness with more or fewer chili peppers
- Serve with steamed rice or noodles

Directions

For the Tofu:
1. Cube the extra-firm tofu and pan-fry until crispy.

For the Lemongrass Chili Sauce:
2. In a separate pan, heat cooking oil over medium heat.
3. Add minced lemongrass, minced garlic, and sliced red chili peppers.
4. Sauté until fragrant.
5. Stir in soy sauce, agave syrup, and lime juice.
6. Add the crispy tofu cubes to the pan and toss to coat in the sauce.
7. Serve hot and enjoy your Vegan Lemongrass Chili Tofu!

4 servings | 220 calories | 30 minutes

Vegan Ginger Tofu and Bok Choy Stir-Fry

Experience the harmonious blend of ginger-infused tofu and vibrant bok choy in this delectable stir-fry.

Ingredients:

For the Stir-Fry:
- 1 block of extra-firm tofu, cubed and fried
- Bok choy, separated into stalks and leaves
- 2 cloves garlic, minced
- 1 thumb-sized piece of ginger, minced
- Sliced red bell pepper
- 2 tbsp soy sauce
- 1 tbsp agave syrup (or sweetener of choice)
- 1 tsp sesame oil
- Salt and pepper to taste
- Cooking oil for stir-frying

Substitutions

- Customize the stir-fry with your favorite vegetables
- Add crushed red pepper flakes for extra heat
- Serve over rice or noodles

Directions

For the Stir-Fry:
1. Cube the extra-firm tofu and pan-fry until crispy.
2. In a wok or large skillet, heat cooking oil over high heat.
3. Add minced garlic and minced ginger, sauté until fragrant.
4. Add bok choy stalks and sliced red bell pepper, stir-fry until slightly tender.
5. Add bok choy leaves and crispy tofu cubes.
6. Drizzle with soy sauce, agave syrup, and sesame oil.
7. Stir-fry until everything is well combined and heated through.
8. Season with salt and pepper to taste.
9. Serve hot and enjoy your Vegan Ginger Tofu and Bok Choy Stir-Fry!

4 servings

180 calories

40 minutes

Vegan Tofu "Shrimp" Cakes

Ingredients:

For the "Shrimp" Cakes:
- 1 block of extra-firm tofu, grated
- Nori seaweed sheets, finely chopped
- 2 cloves garlic, minced
- 1 thumb-sized piece of ginger, minced
- 1/2 tsp Old Bay seasoning (or seafood seasoning of choice)
- Salt and pepper to taste
- Panko breadcrumbs
- Cooking oil for frying

Dipping Sauce:
- Vegan mayonnaise
- Sriracha sauce (adjust to spice preference)

Substitutions

- Adjust the spice level with more or less sriracha
- Serve with a squeeze of fresh lemon juice

Dive into the ocean of flavors with these Vegan Tofu "Shrimp" Cakes, made with tofu, seaweed, and a hint of spice.

Directions

For the "Shrimp" Cakes:
1. Grate the extra-firm tofu and squeeze out excess moisture.
2. In a bowl, combine grated tofu, chopped nori seaweed, minced garlic, minced ginger, Old Bay seasoning, salt, and pepper.
3. Shape the mixture into patties and coat with panko breadcrumbs.
4. Heat cooking oil in a skillet over medium-high heat.
5. Fry the tofu "shrimp" cakes until golden brown on both sides.

Dipping Sauce:
6. Mix vegan mayonnaise with sriracha sauce to taste for the dipping sauce.
7. Serve the "shrimp" cakes hot with the spicy mayo.
8. Enjoy your Vegan Tofu "Shrimp" Cakes!

4 servings | 260 calories | 40 minutes

Vegan Tofu in Black Bean Sauce

Delight in the rich and savory flavors of this Vegan Tofu in Black Bean Sauce, featuring tofu marinated in a velvety black bean sauce with bell peppers and onions.

Ingredients:

For the Tofu:
- 1 block of extra-firm tofu, cubed and fried

For the Black Bean Sauce:
- 3 tbsp black bean sauce
- 2 cloves garlic, minced
- 1 thumb-sized piece of ginger, minced
- Sliced red bell pepper
- Sliced green bell pepper
- Sliced onion
- 1 tbsp soy sauce
- 1 tsp agave syrup (or sweetener of choice)
- Cooking oil for stir-frying

Substitutions

- Customize with your favorite vegetables
- Adjust the sauce's thickness with water
- Garnish with chopped green onions

Directions

For the Tofu:
1. Cube the extra-firm tofu and pan-fry until crispy.

For the Black Bean Sauce:
2. In a wok or large skillet, heat cooking oil over medium-high heat.
3. Add minced garlic and minced ginger, sauté until fragrant.
4. Add sliced red bell pepper, green bell pepper, and onion, stir-fry until slightly tender.
5. Stir in black bean sauce, soy sauce, and agave syrup.
6. Add crispy tofu cubes and toss to coat in the sauce.
7. Serve hot and enjoy your Vegan Tofu in Black Bean Sauce!

4 servings

180 calories

30 minutes

Vegan Tofu and Broccoli in Garlic Sauce

Savor the simplicity of Vegan Tofu and Broccoli in Garlic Sauce, a delightful dish featuring crispy tofu and tender broccoli in a garlicky sauce.

Ingredients:

For the Tofu and Broccoli:
- 1 block of extra-firm tofu, cubed and fried
- Broccoli florets, blanched
- 4 cloves garlic, minced
- Sliced red bell pepper
- Cooking oil for stir-frying

For the Garlic Sauce:
- 3 tbsp soy sauce
- 1 tbsp agave syrup (or sweetener of choice)
- 1 tsp sesame oil
- 2 tsp cornstarch (dissolved in 2 tbsp water)

Substitutions

- Customize with your favorite vegetables
- Adjust the sauce's sweetness and thickness to your taste
- Garnish with sesame seeds or chopped scallions

Directions

For the Tofu and Broccoli:
1. Cube the extra-firm tofu and pan-fry until crispy.
2. In a wok or large skillet, heat cooking oil over medium-high heat.
3. Add minced garlic and stir-fry until fragrant.
4. Add blanched broccoli florets and sliced red bell pepper, stir-fry until heated through.
5. Stir in the garlic sauce mixture and cook until the sauce thickens.
6. Add crispy tofu cubes and toss to coat in the sauce.
7. Serve hot and enjoy your Vegan Tofu and Broccoli in Garlic Sauce!

4 servings | 280 calories | 35 minutes

Vegan Mapo Tofu

Embark on a flavor journey with Vegan Mapo Tofu, a Sichuan-inspired dish featuring tofu and minced mushrooms in a bold and spicy sauce.

Ingredients:

For the Tofu and Mushroom Mix:
- 1 block of extra-firm tofu, cubed and fried
- 1 cup minced mushrooms (shiitake or cremini)

For the Mapo Sauce:
- 3 cloves garlic, minced
- 1 thumb-sized piece of ginger, minced
- 2 tbsp fermented black bean sauce
- 2 tbsp doubanjiang (spicy bean paste, adjust to spice preference)
- 1 tbsp soy sauce
- 1 tsp Sichuan peppercorns, crushed
- 1 tsp agave syrup (or sweetener of choice)
- Cooking oil for stir-frying

Substitutions

- Adjust the spiciness with more or less doubanjiang
- Garnish with chopped scallions and cilantro
- Serve with steamed rice

Directions

For the Tofu and Mushroom Mix:
1. Cube the extra-firm tofu and pan-fry until crispy.
2. In a wok or large skillet, heat cooking oil over medium-high heat.
3. Add minced garlic and minced ginger, sauté until fragrant.
4. Stir in fermented black bean sauce, doubanjiang, and crushed Sichuan peppercorns.
5. Add minced mushrooms and stir-fry until cooked.
6. Add soy sauce and agave syrup, mixing well.
7. Add crispy tofu cubes and gently toss to coat in the sauce.
8. Serve hot and enjoy your Vegan Mapo Tofu!

4 servings

240 calories

45 minutes

Vegan Tofu and Mushroom Hot Pot

Gather around the hot pot and relish the comforting flavors of Vegan Tofu and Mushroom Hot Pot, a communal dish that's perfect for sharing.

Ingredients:

For the Hot Pot:
- Vegetable broth
- Assorted mushrooms (shiitake, enoki, oyster)
- Baby bok choy
- Tofu slices (pre-fried or pan-fried)
- Glass noodles
- Sliced red bell pepper
- Sliced carrot
- Sliced scallions
- Sliced chili peppers (optional)

Dipping Sauce:
- Soy sauce
- Sesame oil
- Sliced garlic
- Sliced ginger

Substitutions

- Customize with your favorite hot pot ingredients
- Adjust the dipping sauce to your taste
- Provide a variety of dipping sauces for a fun hot pot experience

Directions

For the Hot Pot:
1. Prepare a pot of vegetable broth and bring it to a simmer at the dining table.
2. Arrange assorted mushrooms, baby bok choy, tofu slices, glass noodles, sliced red bell pepper, sliced carrot, sliced scallions, and sliced chili peppers (if desired) on the table.
3. Each diner can add their desired ingredients to the simmering broth and cook to their preference.

Dipping Sauce:
4. Mix soy sauce, sesame oil, sliced garlic, and sliced ginger for a dipping sauce.
5. Enjoy your Vegan Tofu and Mushroom Hot Pot!

4 servings   230 calories   35 minutes

Vegan Tofu and Eggplant Stir-Fry

Ingredients:

For the Stir-Fry:
- 1 block of extra-firm tofu, cubed and fried
- Eggplant, sliced and prepped
- 2 cloves garlic, minced
- Sliced red bell pepper
- Cooking oil for stir-frying

For the Stir-Fry Sauce:
- 3 tbsp soy sauce
- 1 tbsp agave syrup (or sweetener of choice)
- 1 tsp sesame oil
- 2 tsp cornstarch (dissolved in 2 tbsp water)

Substitutions

- Customize with your favorite vegetables
- Adjust the sauce's sweetness and thickness to your taste
- Garnish with chopped cilantro

Indulge in the medley of flavors in this Vegan Tofu and Eggplant Stir-Fry, where tender eggplant and crispy tofu are coated in a savory sauce.

Directions

For the Stir-Fry:
1. Cube the extra-firm tofu and pan-fry until crispy.
2. In a wok or large skillet, heat cooking oil over medium-high heat.
3. Add minced garlic and stir-fry until fragrant.
4. Add sliced eggplant and stir-fry until slightly tender.
5. Add sliced red bell pepper and continue to stir-fry until heated through.
6. In a small bowl, combine soy sauce, agave syrup, sesame oil, and cornstarch mixture.
7. Pour the sauce over the stir-fry and cook until the sauce thickens.
8. Add crispy tofu cubes and gently toss to coat in the sauce.
9. Serve hot and enjoy your Vegan Tofu and Eggplant Stir-Fry!

4 servings

190 calories

30 minutes

Vegan Tofu Satay Skewers

Delight in the smoky and savory goodness of these Vegan Tofu Satay Skewers, served with a rich and creamy peanut sauce.

Ingredients:

For the Tofu Satay:
- 1 block of extra-firm tofu, cubed and marinated
- Wooden skewers, soaked in water

For the Peanut Sauce:
- 1/2 cup peanut butter
- 2 tbsp soy sauce
- 1 tbsp agave syrup (or sweetener of choice)
- Juice of 1 lime
- 2 cloves garlic, minced
- Sliced chili peppers (optional)
- Water to adjust consistency

Substitutions

- Customize the marinade with your favorite flavors
- Adjust the peanut sauce's spiciness with chili peppers
- Drizzle with fresh cilantro for garnish

Directions

For the Tofu Satay:
1. Cube the extra-firm tofu and marinate in your choice of marinade.
2. Thread the marinated tofu onto soaked wooden skewers.
3. Grill or pan-fry the tofu skewers until lightly charred.

For the Peanut Sauce:
4. In a bowl, whisk together peanut butter, soy sauce, agave syrup, lime juice, minced garlic, and sliced chili peppers (if desired).
5. Add water to achieve your desired sauce consistency.
6. Serve the tofu skewers with the peanut sauce for dipping.
7. Enjoy your Vegan Tofu Satay Skewers!

4 servings

200 calories

30 minutes

Vegan Tofu and Asparagus Stir-Fry

Experience the vibrant combination of tofu and asparagus in this quick and easy stir-fry.

Ingredients:

For the Stir-Fry:
- 1 block of extra-firm tofu, cubed and fried
- Asparagus spears, trimmed and cut into pieces
- 2 cloves garlic, minced
- Sliced red bell pepper
- Cooking oil for stir-frying

For the Stir-Fry Sauce:
- 3 tbsp soy sauce
- 1 tbsp agave syrup (or sweetener of choice)
- 1 tsp sesame oil
- 2 tsp cornstarch (dissolved in 2 tbsp water)

Substitutions

- Customize with your favorite vegetables
- Adjust the sauce's sweetness and thickness to your taste
- Garnish with toasted sesame seeds

Directions

For the Stir-Fry:
1. Cube the extra-firm tofu and pan-fry until crispy.
2. In a wok or large skillet, heat cooking oil over medium-high heat.
3. Add minced garlic and stir-fry until fragrant.
4. Add asparagus pieces and stir-fry until tender-crisp.
5. Add sliced red bell pepper and continue to stir-fry until heated through.
6. In a small bowl, combine soy sauce, agave syrup, sesame oil, and cornstarch mixture.
7. Pour the sauce over the stir-fry and cook until the sauce thickens.
8. Add crispy tofu cubes and gently toss to coat in the sauce.
9. Serve hot and enjoy your Vegan Tofu and Asparagus Stir-Fry!

We need your support

As we find ourselves in the midst of the "Vietnamese Vegan Cookbook," I want to take a pause in our culinary journey and talk about something that's near and dear to us – your feedback. In the world of small publishers like us, reviews are as elusive and precious as the perfect bowl of pho.

If you've been savoring the flavors of our plant-based Vietnamese recipes, if you've found authenticity and simplicity in our dishes made from easy-to-find ingredients, I'd like to ask for your support. Your review is more than just a comment; it's a lifeline for us.

Please take a moment to return to the app or website where you acquired this book. There, you'll discover that cherished review button. Give us a rating and share a few sentences about your experience. Your review isn't just a gesture; it's a connection. It guides other culinary explorers to these pages, and it fuels our passion for bringing Vietnamese vegan cuisine to your kitchen.

Every review you leave is like a sprig of fresh herbs that flavors our commitment to creating authentic and accessible recipes. We read each one with genuine appreciation and eagerness to learn from your insights and experiences.

And if, by any chance, you've encountered a minor hiccup or oversight along the way, please understand that we've poured our heart and soul into crafting this culinary journey. Despite our dedication, even the most meticulous chefs can occasionally encounter bumps in the road. Your understanding is the sriracha that adds a spicy kick to our journey.

Now, let's return to what truly matters – the recipes that beckon us back to the vibrant flavors of Vietnam. Your next culinary adventure awaits, and we're excited to share it with you. Thank you for being a part of this flavorful exploration, and let's continue creating authentic and delicious Vietnamese vegan dishes together.

Chapter 5:
Hearty Soups and Stews

4 servings

300 calories

45 minutes

Vegan Phở Bò (Pho with Beef)

Warm your soul with this Vegan Phở Bò, a Vietnamese noodle soup brimming with aromatic herbs, rice noodles, and hearty plant-based beef.

Ingredients:

For the Broth:
- Vegan beef broth
- Star anise, cloves, and cinnamon sticks
- Sliced ginger
- Chopped lemongrass
- Soy sauce
- Agave syrup (or sweetener of choice)
- Salt and pepper to taste

For the Soup:
- Rice noodles
- Vegan beef slices
- Bean sprouts
- Fresh herbs (Thai basil, cilantro, mint)
- Lime wedges
- Sliced chili peppers (optional)

Substitutions

- Customize with your favorite herbs and toppings
- Adjust the spiciness with more or fewer chili peppers
- Add sriracha sauce for extra heat

Directions

For the Broth:
1. In a large pot, simmer vegan beef broth with star anise, cloves, cinnamon sticks, sliced ginger, chopped lemongrass, soy sauce, agave syrup, salt, and pepper.

For the Soup:
2. Cook rice noodles according to package instructions and drain.
3. In serving bowls, layer cooked rice noodles, vegan beef slices, and bean sprouts.
4. Pour hot broth over the noodles and top with fresh herbs, lime wedges, and sliced chili peppers (if desired).
5. Enjoy your Vegan Phở Bò!

4 servings

260 calories

35 minutes

Vegan Canh Bún (Rice Noodle Soup)

Dive into a bowl of Vegan Canh Bún, a Vietnamese rice noodle soup loaded with tofu, fresh vegetables, and aromatic broth.

Ingredients:

For the Broth:
- Vegetable broth
- Sliced ginger
- Soy sauce
- Agave syrup (or sweetener of choice)
- Salt and pepper to taste

For the Soup:
- Rice vermicelli
- Cubed tofu, pan-fried
- Bean sprouts
- Sliced cucumber
- Fresh herbs (cilantro, mint, Thai basil)
- Crushed peanuts
- Lime wedges
- Sliced chili peppers (optional)

Substitutions

- Customize with your favorite vegetables and herbs
- Adjust the spiciness with more or fewer chili peppers
- Drizzle with hoisin sauce for added flavor

Directions

For the Broth:
1. In a pot, bring vegetable broth to a simmer with sliced ginger, soy sauce, agave syrup, salt, and pepper.

For the Soup:
2. Cook rice vermicelli according to package instructions and drain.
3. In serving bowls, layer cooked rice vermicelli, cubed pan-fried tofu, and bean sprouts.
4. Pour hot broth over the noodles and toppings.
5. Top with sliced cucumber, fresh herbs, crushed peanuts, lime wedges, and sliced chili peppers (if desired).
6. Enjoy your Vegan Canh Bún!

4 servings

290 calories

50 minutes

Vegan Hủ tiếu Nam Vang (Cambodian Noodle Soup)

Discover the flavors of Cambodia with Vegan Hủ tiếu Nam Vang, a fragrant noodle soup featuring rice noodles, vegan "shrimp," and a savory broth.

Ingredients:

For the Broth:
- Vegan chicken broth
- Sliced ginger
- Soy sauce
- Agave syrup (or sweetener of choice)
- Salt and pepper to taste

For the Soup:
- Rice noodles
- Vegan "shrimp"
- Bean sprouts
- Fresh herbs (cilantro, mint, Thai basil)
- Lime wedges
- Sliced chili peppers (optional)

Substitutions

- Customize with your favorite toppings and herbs
- Adjust the spiciness with more or fewer chili peppers
- Add garlic chili sauce for extra heat

Directions

For the Broth:
1. In a pot, bring vegan chicken broth to a simmer with sliced ginger, soy sauce, agave syrup, salt, and pepper.

For the Soup:
2. Cook rice noodles according to package instructions and drain.
3. In serving bowls, layer cooked rice noodles, vegan "shrimp," and bean sprouts.
4. Pour hot broth over the noodles and toppings.
5. Top with fresh herbs, lime wedges, and sliced chili peppers (if desired).
6. Enjoy your Vegan Hủ tiếu Nam Vang!

4 servings

220 calories

30 minutes

Vegan Cá Nướng (Grilled "Fish")

Experience the delightful flavors of Vegan Cá Nướng, where marinated tofu is grilled to perfection, mimicking the taste of grilled fish.

Ingredients:

For the Marinade:
- Soy sauce
- Minced garlic
- Minced lemongrass
- Agave syrup (or sweetener of choice)
- Sliced chili peppers (optional)
- Salt and pepper to taste

For Grilling:
- Extra-firm tofu slices
- Banana leaves (or aluminum foil)

Dipping Sauce:
- Soy sauce
- Lime juice
- Sliced chili peppers (optional)

Substitutions

- Customize the marinade with your favorite flavors
- Adjust the spiciness with more or fewer chili peppers
- Garnish with fresh herbs

Directions

For the Marinade:
1. In a bowl, mix soy sauce, minced garlic, minced lemongrass, agave syrup, sliced chili peppers (if desired), salt, and pepper.
2. Marinate extra-firm tofu slices in the mixture for at least 15 minutes.

For Grilling:
3. Place marinated tofu slices on banana leaves (or aluminum foil).
4. Grill until both sides are charred and aromatic.

Dipping Sauce:
5. Mix soy sauce, lime juice, and sliced chili peppers (if desired) for a dipping sauce.
6. Serve the grilled "fish" with the dipping sauce.
7. Enjoy your Vegan Cá Nướng!

4 servings | 320 calories | 60 minutes

Vegan Bò Kho (Beef Stew)

Warm your heart with Vegan Bò Kho, a Vietnamese-inspired beef stew made with tender seitan, carrots, and aromatic spices.

Ingredients:

For the Stew:
- Seitan chunks
- Chopped onions
- Minced garlic
- Minced lemongrass
- Soy sauce
- Tomato paste
- Five-spice powder
- Ground annatto seeds (optional for color)
- Vegetable broth
- Chopped carrots and potatoes
- Coconut milk (optional for creaminess)
- Salt and pepper to taste

For Serving:
- Fresh herbs (cilantro, Thai basil)
- Lime wedges
- Baguette or rice noodles

Substitutions

- Customize with your favorite vegetables and herbs
- Adjust the spice level to your taste
- Serve with your preferred side (baguette or rice noodles)

Directions

For the Stew:
1. In a large pot, sauté chopped onions, minced garlic, and minced lemongrass until fragrant.
2. Add seitan chunks and sear briefly.
3. Stir in soy sauce, tomato paste, five-spice powder, ground annatto seeds (if using), and vegetable broth.
4. Add chopped carrots and potatoes and simmer until tender.
5. Optionally, add coconut milk for creaminess.
6. Season with salt and pepper to taste.

For Serving:
7. Serve the stew with fresh herbs, lime wedges, and baguette or rice noodles.
8. Enjoy your Vegan Bò Kho!

4 servings | 160 calories | 25 minutes

Vegan Canh Cải (Mustard Green Soup)

Enjoy the simplicity of Vegan Canh Cải, a Vietnamese mustard green soup bursting with fresh flavors and tender greens.

Ingredients:

For the Soup:
- Mustard greens, chopped
- Sliced ginger
- Vegetable broth
- Soy sauce
- Salt and pepper to taste

For Serving:
- Cooked rice

Directions

For the Soup:
1. In a pot, bring vegetable broth to a simmer with sliced ginger, soy sauce, salt, and pepper.
2. Add chopped mustard greens and cook until wilted but still vibrant.

For Serving:
3. Serve the soup with a side of cooked rice.
4. Enjoy your Vegan Canh Cải!

Substitutions

- Customize with your favorite greens
- Add tofu or mushrooms for extra protein
- Garnish with fresh herbs

4 servings | 240 calories | 40 minutes

Vegan Bún Măng (Bamboo Shoot Noodle Soup)

Delight in the unique flavors of Vegan Bún Măng, a Vietnamese noodle soup featuring bamboo shoots and tofu in a fragrant broth.

Ingredients:

For the Broth:
- Vegetable broth
- Sliced ginger
- Soy sauce
- Agave syrup (or sweetener of choice)
- Salt and pepper to taste
- Bamboo shoots

For the Soup:
- Rice vermicelli
- Cubed tofu, pan-fried
- Bean sprouts
- Fresh herbs (cilantro, mint, Thai basil)
- Lime wedges
- Sliced chili peppers (optional)

Substitutions

- Customize with your favorite toppings and herbs
- Adjust the spiciness with more or fewer chili peppers
- Drizzle with hoisin sauce for added flavor

Directions

For the Broth:
1. In a pot, bring vegetable broth to a simmer with sliced ginger, soy sauce, agave syrup, salt, pepper, and bamboo shoots.

For the Soup:
2. Cook rice vermicelli according to package instructions and drain.
3. In serving bowls, layer cooked rice vermicelli, cubed pan-fried tofu, and bean sprouts.
4. Pour hot broth over the noodles and toppings.
5. Top with fresh herbs, lime wedges, and sliced chili peppers (if desired).
6. Enjoy your Vegan Bún Măng!

4 servings

280 calories

40 minutes

Vegan Hủ tiếu Khô (Dry Noodles with Sauce)

Savor the rich and flavorful Vegan Hủ tiếu Kho, a Vietnamese dish featuring dry noodles topped with a savory sauce, tofu, and herbs.

Ingredients:

For the Sauce:
- Soy sauce
- Minced garlic
- Minced lemongrass
- Agave syrup (or sweetener of choice)
- Sliced chili peppers (optional)
- Salt and pepper to taste

For Serving:
- Rice noodles
- Cubed tofu, pan-fried
- Bean sprouts
- Fresh herbs (cilantro, mint, Thai basil)
- Lime wedges

Substitutions

- Customize with your favorite toppings and herbs
- Adjust the spiciness with more or fewer chili peppers
- Drizzle with hoisin sauce for added flavor

Directions

For the Sauce:
1. In a bowl, mix soy sauce, minced garlic, minced lemongrass, agave syrup, sliced chili peppers (if desired), salt, and pepper.
2. Adjust the seasoning to your taste.

For Serving:
3. Cook rice noodles according to package instructions and drain.
4. In serving bowls, layer cooked rice noodles, cubed pan-fried tofu, and bean sprouts.
5. Drizzle the sauce over the noodles and toppings.
6. Top with fresh herbs and serve with lime wedges.
7. Enjoy your Vegan Hủ tiếu Kho!

4 servings

180 calories

40 minutes

Vegan Cháo (Congee with Tofu)

Embrace comfort with Vegan Cháo, a Vietnamese congee featuring silky tofu and aromatic toppings, perfect for soothing any soul.

Ingredients:

For the Congee:
- Rice
- Vegetable broth
- Sliced ginger
- Minced garlic
- Cubed silken tofu
- Soy sauce
- Salt and pepper to taste

For Toppings:
- Sliced scallions
- Fried shallots
- Sliced chili peppers (optional)
- Lime wedges

Directions

For the Congee:
1. In a pot, bring rice, vegetable broth, sliced ginger, minced garlic, and salt to a simmer.
2. Cook until the rice is soft and the congee reaches your desired consistency.
3. Add cubed silken tofu, soy sauce, salt, and pepper.

For Toppings:
4. Serve the congee hot with sliced scallions, fried shallots, sliced chili peppers (if desired), and lime wedges.
5. Enjoy your Vegan Cháo!

Substitutions

- Customize with your favorite toppings
- Adjust the spiciness with more or fewer chili peppers
- Garnish with fresh herbs

4 servings

100 calories

20 minutes

Vegan Cải Xào (Stir-Fried Mustard Greens)

Elevate your greens with Vegan Cải Xào, a simple yet flavorful Vietnamese stir-fry featuring mustard greens and garlic.

Ingredients:

For the Stir-Fry:
- Mustard greens, chopped
- Minced garlic
- Cooking oil
- Soy sauce
- Salt and pepper to taste

Directions

For the Stir-Fry:
1. Heat cooking oil in a pan or wok over medium-high heat.
2. Add minced garlic and sauté until fragrant.
3. Add chopped mustard greens and stir-fry until wilted but still vibrant.
4. Season with soy sauce, salt, and pepper to taste.
5. Serve hot and enjoy your Vegan Cải Xào!

Substitutions

- Customize with your favorite greens
- Add tofu or mushrooms for extra protein
- Garnish with toasted sesame seeds

Chapter 6:
Fresh and Vibrant Salads

4 rolls

120 calories

25 mins

Vegan Gỏi Cuốn

These fresh spring rolls are a vegan twist on a Vietnamese classic. Delicate rice paper wraps filled with crunchy veggies and tofu, served with a zesty dipping sauce.

Ingredients:

- 4 rice paper sheets
- 1 cup tofu, julienned
- 1 cup lettuce, shredded
- 1 cup bean sprouts
- Fresh herbs (mint, cilantro)
- Rice noodles
- Dipping sauce

Directions

1. Soak rice paper in warm water.
2. Assemble veggies, tofu, and herbs on rice paper.
3. Roll tightly and serve with dipping sauce.

2 servings

150 calories

15 mins

Vegan Green Papaya Salad

This vegan version of the classic green papaya salad is a burst of flavors and textures. A tangy dressing brings out the best in shredded green papaya and peanuts.

Ingredients:

- 2 cups shredded green papaya
- 1/4 cup peanuts
- Fresh herbs (Thai basil, cilantro)
- 1-2 red chili peppers
- Dressing (lime juice, soy sauce, sugar)

Directions

1. Prepare dressing by mixing lime juice, soy sauce, and sugar.
2. Toss shredded papaya, herbs, and peanuts with the dressing.
3. Garnish with chili peppers.

4 servings   130 calories   20 mins

Vegan Mango Salad

This vegan mango salad is a tropical delight. Sweet mangoes, crunchy vegetables, and a zesty dressing create a harmonious and refreshing dish.

Ingredients:

- 2 ripe mangoes, diced
- 1 cucumber, julienned
- 1 red bell pepper, thinly sliced
- Fresh herbs (mint, basil)
- Peanuts
- Dressing (lime juice, soy sauce, chili)

Directions

1. Whisk together lime juice, soy sauce, and chili for the dressing.
2. Toss mangoes, cucumber, and bell pepper in the dressing.
3. Garnish with herbs and peanuts.

2 servings

90 calories

15 mins

Vegan Water Spinach Salad

This vegan water spinach salad is a quick and healthy dish. Stir-fried water spinach with garlic and a savory sauce creates a simple yet flavorful side.

Ingredients:

- 1 bunch water spinach
- 2 cloves garlic, minced
- Soy sauce
- Sesame oil
- Salt and pepper

Directions

1. Heat sesame oil in a pan, add garlic, and stir-fry until fragrant.
2. Add water spinach and cook until wilted.
3. Season with soy sauce, salt, and pepper.

4 servings

60 calories

10 mins

Vegan Cucumber Salad

This vegan cucumber salad is a crisp and cool side dish. Sliced cucumbers are marinated in a tangy dressing with a hint of spice for a refreshing bite.

Ingredients:

- 2 cucumbers, thinly sliced
- 1 red onion, thinly sliced
- 1/4 cup rice vinegar
- 2 tbsp sugar
- Red chili flakes
- Fresh dill (optional)

Directions

1. Mix rice vinegar, sugar, and chili flakes for the dressing.
2. Toss cucumbers and onions in the dressing.
3. Chill before serving, garnish with dill.

2 servings   180 calories   30 mins

Vegan Tofu Salad

This vegan tofu salad is protein-packed and full of flavor. Marinated tofu is pan-fried to perfection and served with a bed of fresh greens and herbs.

Ingredients:

- 1 block of tofu, cubed
- Mixed greens
- Fresh herbs (mint, cilantro)
- Dressing (soy sauce, sesame oil, garlic, lime juice)
- Crushed peanuts

Directions

1. Marinate tofu in dressing for 15 mins, then pan-fry until crispy.
2. Arrange tofu on greens and herbs.
3. Garnish with crushed peanuts.

4 servings **140 calories** **25 mins**

Vegan Pomelo Salad

This vegan pomelo salad is a burst of citrusy goodness. Sweet pomelo segments are paired with shrimp-like tofu and a zesty dressing for a tropical treat.

Ingredients:

- 1 pomelo, peeled and segmented
- 1/2 cup tofu, diced
- Fresh herbs (mint, basil)
- Crushed peanuts
- Dressing (lime juice, soy sauce, sugar, chili)

Directions

1. Mix lime juice, soy sauce, sugar, and chili for the dressing.
2. Toss pomelo, tofu, and herbs in the dressing.
3. Top with crushed peanuts.

2 servings

110 calories

20 mins

Vegan Grapefruit Salad

This vegan grapefruit salad is a symphony of flavors. Juicy grapefruit, avocado, and greens come together with a zesty dressing for a refreshing appetizer.

Ingredients:

- 1 grapefruit, segmented
- 1 avocado, diced
- Mixed greens
- Dressing (olive oil, balsamic vinegar, Dijon mustard, maple syrup)
- Salt and pepper

Directions

1. Whisk together dressing ingredients, season with salt and pepper.
2. Toss grapefruit, avocado, and greens in the dressing.
3. Serve chilled.

4 servings

190 calories

15 mins

Vegan Avocado Salad

This vegan avocado salad is creamy and satisfying. Ripe avocados, tomatoes, and red onions are tossed in a cilantro-lime dressing for a flavorful side.

Ingredients:

- 2 ripe avocados, diced
- 2 tomatoes, diced
- 1/2 red onion, thinly sliced
- Fresh cilantro
- Dressing (lime juice, olive oil, garlic, salt)

Directions

1. Mix lime juice, olive oil, and garlic for the dressing.
2. Toss avocados, tomatoes, and onions in the dressing.
3. Garnish with cilantro.

2 servings   40 calories   10 mins

Vegan Mixed Herb Salad

This vegan mixed herb salad is a fragrant and light side dish. A medley of fresh herbs, dressed with a simple vinaigrette, adds a burst of flavor to any meal.

Ingredients:

- Fresh herbs (mint, basil, cilantro, Thai basil)
- Dressing (lime juice, soy sauce, sugar, chili)

Directions

1. Whisk together lime juice, soy sauce, sugar, and chili for the dressing.
2. Toss the mixed herbs in the dressing until well coated.
3. Serve immediately.

Chapter 7:
Noodle Extravaganza

4 bowls   350   45 mins

Vegan Bún Bò Huế (Spicy Noodle Soup)

A vegan twist on the famous spicy beef noodle soup from Huế. This rich and flavorful broth will awaken your taste buds.

Ingredients:

- 8 oz rice vermicelli noodles
- 1 cup sliced mushrooms
- 1 cup tofu cubes
- 2 tbsp vegan fish sauce
- 2 tbsp lemongrass (minced)
- 1 tbsp red chili paste
- 6 cups vegetable broth
- 1 cup bean sprouts
- Fresh herbs (cilantro, mint, Thai basil)
- Lime wedges

Directions

1. In a pot, sauté mushrooms, tofu, lemongrass, and chili paste until fragrant.
2. Add vegetable broth and simmer for 30 mins.
3. Cook noodles separately.
4. Assemble bowls with noodles, broth, and toppings.
5. Serve with lime wedges.

4 bowls   280   30 mins

Vegan Bánh Canh Chả Cá (Fish Cake Noodle Soup)

Dive into the comfort of this fish cake noodle soup without harming any fish. The creamy broth and tender "fish" cakes will win your heart.

Ingredients:

- 10 oz rice udon noodles
- 1 cup vegan fish cakes
- 4 cups vegetable broth
- 1 cup coconut milk
- 1 tsp turmeric
- 2 cloves garlic (minced)
- 1 tbsp scallions (chopped)
- Fresh herbs (cilantro, basil)
- Lime wedges

Directions

1. In a pot, simmer vegetable broth and coconut milk with turmeric.
2. Add vegan fish cakes and cook for 15 mins.
3. Cook noodles separately.
4. Serve noodles in broth with herbs and lime wedges.

4 bowls | 320 | 50 mins

Vegan Bánh Canh Giò Heo (Pork Knuckle Noodle Soup)

This noodle soup captures the essence of pork knuckle soup, but cruelty-free. The savory broth and tender "pork" will leave you craving more.

Ingredients:

- 12 oz wide rice noodles
- 1 cup vegan pork knuckles
- 6 cups vegetable broth
- 1 tbsp soy sauce
- 1 tsp five-spice powder
- 2 cloves garlic (minced)
- 1 cup bok choy (chopped)
- 1 tbsp fried shallots
- Fresh herbs (cilantro, Thai basil)
- Lime wedges

Directions

1. In a pot, simmer vegetable broth with soy sauce and five-spice powder.
2. Add vegan pork knuckles and cook for 30 mins.
3. Cook noodles separately.
4. Serve with bok choy, herbs, and lime wedges.

4 servings | 280 | 40 mins

Vegan Mì Quảng (Turmeric Noodles)

Mì Quảng is a vibrant noodle dish from central Vietnam. This vegan version features turmeric-infused noodles, fresh herbs, and roasted peanuts.

Ingredients:

- 8 oz turmeric rice noodles
- 1 cup tofu (sliced)
- 1 cup mushrooms (sliced)
- 2 cups vegetable broth
- 2 tbsp turmeric powder
- 1 tsp garlic (minced)
- Fresh herbs (cilantro, mint, basil)
- Roasted peanuts
- Lime wedges

Directions

1. Cook rice noodles and set aside.
2. Sauté tofu and mushrooms until golden.
3. Boil vegetable broth with turmeric and garlic.
4. Assemble bowls with noodles, tofu, and broth.
5. Garnish with herbs, peanuts, and lime wedges.

4 bowls   290   35 mins

Vegan Bún Rieu Cua (Crab Noodle Soup)

A delightful vegan rendition of the classic crab noodle soup. The tomato-based broth and tofu "crab" patties make this dish a winner.

Ingredients:

- 10 oz rice vermicelli noodles
- 1 cup tofu "crab" patties
- 4 cups vegetable broth
- 1 cup tomatoes (diced)
- 1 cup tamarind broth
- 2 tbsp vegan fish sauce
- 1 tsp shrimp paste (optional)
- Fresh herbs (cilantro, mint, Thai basil)
- Lime wedges

Directions

1. Cook noodles and set aside.
2. In a pot, simmer vegetable broth, tomatoes, tamarind, and seasonings.
3. Add tofu "crab" patties and cook for 15 mins.
4. Serve noodles in broth with herbs and lime wedges.

Substitutions

Vegan fish sauce

4 bowls

260

40 mins

Vegan Bún Măng Vịt (Duck Bamboo Shoot Noodle Soup)

Normal

A comforting noodle soup with tender "duck" and bamboo shoots. The savory broth will transport you to the streets of Vietnam.

Ingredients:

- 8 oz rice vermicelli noodles
- 1 cup vegan duck slices
- 1 cup bamboo shoots (sliced)
- 6 cups vegetable broth
- 2 tbsp soy sauce
- 2 cloves garlic (minced)
- Fresh herbs (cilantro, Thai basil)
- Lime wedges

Directions

1. Cook noodles separately and set aside.
2. Sauté vegan duck and bamboo shoots with soy sauce and garlic.
3. Simmer vegetable broth.
4. Assemble bowls with noodles, "duck," and broth.
5. Garnish with herbs and lime wedges.

4 bowls | 250 | 40 mins

Vegan Bún Riêu Chay (Vegan Crab Noodle Soup)

A cruelty-free twist on the beloved crab noodle soup. The tofu "crab" patties and tomato-based broth are simply divine.

Ingredients:

- 10 oz rice vermicelli noodles
- 1 cup tofu "crab" patties
- 4 cups vegetable broth
- 1 cup tomatoes (diced)
- 1 cup tomato paste
- 2 tbsp vegan fish sauce
- 2 tbsp tamarind concentrate
- Fresh herbs (cilantro, mint, Thai basil)
- Lime wedges

Directions

1. Cook noodles and set aside.
2. In a pot, simmer vegetable broth, tomatoes, tomato paste, and seasonings.
3. Add tofu "crab" patties and cook for 15 mins.
4. Serve noodles in broth with herbs and lime wedges.

Substitutions

Vegan fish sauce

4 servings   240   25 mins

Vegan Bánh Đa Cua (Crab Noodle Salad)

A refreshing crab noodle salad with a zesty vegan twist. Perfect for a light and satisfying meal on a hot day.

Ingredients:

- 8 oz bánh đa (rice crackers)
- 1 cup shredded vegan crab
- 1 cup cucumber (julienned)
- 1 cup lettuce (shredded)
- 2 tbsp vegan fish sauce
- 2 tbsp lime juice
- 1 tsp chili garlic sauce
- 2 cloves garlic (minced)
- Crushed peanuts

Directions

1. Crush bánh đa into bite-sized pieces.
2. Mix vegan crab, cucumber, and lettuce.
3. In a bowl, combine vegan fish sauce, lime juice, chili sauce, and garlic.
4. Toss the salad with the dressing.
5. Garnish with crushed peanuts.

4 servings

280

30 mins

Vegan Bún Thịt Nướng (Grilled "Meat" Noodles)

Enjoy the flavors of Vietnam with these grilled "meat" noodles. Marinated tofu and a sweet-tangy sauce make it irresistible.

Ingredients:

- 8 oz rice vermicelli noodles
- 1 cup grilled tofu (sliced)
- 1 cup shredded lettuce
- 1 cup bean sprouts
- 1 cup fresh herbs (cilantro, mint, Thai basil)
- 2 tbsp vegan fish sauce
- 2 tbsp hoisin sauce
- Crushed peanuts
- Lime wedges

Directions

1. Cook noodles and set aside.
2. Marinate tofu in vegan fish sauce and hoisin sauce.
3. Grill tofu until slightly charred.
4. Assemble bowls with noodles, tofu, veggies, and herbs.
5. Garnish with peanuts and lime wedges.

4 bowls   **240**   **35 mins**

Vegan Bún Mì (Egg Noodle Soup)

A comforting egg noodle soup made entirely vegan. The silky noodles and flavorful broth will warm your heart.

Ingredients:

- 8 oz vegan egg noodles
- 1 cup tofu (cubed)
- 4 cups vegetable broth
- 1 cup bok choy (chopped)
- 1 tsp ginger (minced)
- 2 cloves garlic (minced)
- 2 tbsp soy sauce
- 1 tsp sesame oil
- Fresh herbs (cilantro, green onions)
- Lime wedges

Directions

1. Cook egg noodles and set aside.
2. Sauté tofu, ginger, and garlic.
3. Boil vegetable broth with soy sauce and sesame oil.
4. Assemble bowls with noodles, tofu, bok choy, and herbs.
5. Serve with lime wedges.

Chapter 8:
Street Food Favorites

2 servings | 300 | 30 mins

Vegan Bánh Mì Chảo (Sizzling Crepe)

This sizzling crepe is a Vietnamese street food classic! Crispy on the outside, tender on the inside, and bursting with flavor. Enjoy the delightful dance of textures and tastes.

Ingredients:

- 1 cup rice flour
- 1/4 cup coconut milk
- 1/2 cup water
- 1/4 tsp turmeric powder
- 1/2 cup mung bean sprouts
- 1/2 cup tofu, thinly sliced
- 2-3 green onions, chopped
- Soy sauce
- Cooking oil
- Vegan fish sauce
- Lettuce leaves
- Fresh herbs (mint, cilantro)
- Dipping sauce (hoisin and peanut sauce)
- Chili slices (optional)

Directions

1. In a bowl, mix rice flour, coconut milk, water, and turmeric powder until smooth.
2. Heat a non-stick pan, add oil, and sauté tofu until golden brown. Set aside.
3. Pour a ladle of the rice flour mixture into the pan, swirling to coat evenly. Add bean sprouts, green onions, and tofu.
4. Cover and cook until crispy.
5. Fold in half and serve with lettuce, herbs, dipping sauce, and chili.
6. Enjoy your sizzling crepe!

2 servings   350   20 mins

Vegan Bánh Mì Hòa Mã (Mixed Baguette)

A delightful fusion of flavors in a crusty baguette. Perfect for a quick, satisfying meal on the go.

Ingredients:

- 1 vegan baguette
- Vegan mayonnaise
- Vegan pâté
- Vegan ham or tofu slices
- Cucumber slices
- Pickled daikon and carrots
- Fresh cilantro
- Jalapeño slices (optional)

Directions

1. Slice the baguette in half and lightly toast it.
2. Spread vegan mayonnaise and pâté on both sides.
3. Layer with vegan ham or tofu, cucumber, pickled daikon, carrots, cilantro, and jalapeño.
4. Close the sandwich and enjoy this savory delight!

2 servings | 320 | 15 mins

Vegan Bánh Mì Kẹp (Sandwiches)

Simple yet satisfying, these sandwiches are a Vietnamese favorite. Customize with your favorite fillings.

Ingredients:

- 1 baguette or bread of choice
- Vegan mayonnaise
- Vegan butter
- Vegan protein (tofu, tempeh, seitan, or mock meats)
- Fresh vegetables (lettuce, cucumber, tomato)
- Vegan cheese slices (optional)
- Pickles
- Soy sauce or hot sauce (optional)

Directions

1. Slice the baguette or bread and spread vegan mayonnaise and vegan butter.
2. Cook the vegan protein until crispy and season with soy sauce or hot sauce if desired.
3. Assemble your sandwich with protein, fresh veggies, vegan cheese, and pickles.
4. Serve and savor the flavors!

2 servings | 280 | 15 mins

Vegan Bánh Mì Nướng (Grilled Baguette)

Grilled baguette with a savory twist. The perfect balance of crispy and chewy textures.

Ingredients:

- 1 baguette
- Vegan garlic butter
- Vegan pâté
- Vegan protein (tofu, tempeh, or seitan)
- Fresh herbs (cilantro, basil)
- Chili slices (optional)

Directions

1. Slice the baguette and spread vegan garlic butter and pâté.
2. Grill or toast until crispy.
3. Grill the vegan protein until golden and slice into strips.
4. Assemble the sandwich with protein, fresh herbs, and chili slices if desired.
5. Enjoy your grilled baguette!

2 servings | 280 | 20 mins

Vegan Bánh Mì Pâté Chay (Vegan Pâté Sandwich)

Indulge in the rich, creamy goodness of this vegan pâté sandwich. A Vietnamese classic made cruelty-free and delicious.

Ingredients:

- 1 baguette or bread of choice
- Vegan pâté
- Vegan mayonnaise
- Vegan deli slices (smoked tofu or tempeh)
- Fresh vegetables (cucumber, lettuce, tomato)
- Fresh herbs (cilantro, mint)
- Pickled daikon and carrots
- Chili slices (optional)

Directions

1. Slice the baguette or bread and spread vegan pâté and vegan mayonnaise.
2. Layer with vegan deli slices, fresh veggies, herbs, pickled daikon, and carrots.
3. Add chili slices for a kick if desired.
4. Assemble your sandwich and relish the flavors!

2 servings | 360 | 40 mins

Vegan Bánh Mì Xiu Mai (Meatball Sandwich)

These savory vegan meatball sandwiches are packed with flavor and texture. A delightful twist on a classic Vietnamese dish.

Ingredients:

- 1 baguette or bread of choice
- Vegan meatballs
- Vegan pâté
- Vegan mayonnaise
- Fresh cilantro
- Pickled daikon and carrots
- Soy sauce or hot sauce (optional)

Directions

1. Cook the vegan meatballs according to package instructions.
2. Slice the baguette and spread vegan pâté and vegan mayonnaise.
3. Layer with meatballs, fresh cilantro, and pickled daikon and carrots.
4. Add soy sauce or hot sauce for extra flavor if desired.
5. Enjoy your meatball sandwich!

4 servings | 160 | 20 mins

Vegan Bánh Tráng Nướng (Grilled Rice Paper)

Easy

Crispy, flavorful, and oh-so-addictive! These grilled rice paper sheets are a beloved Vietnamese street snack.

Ingredients:

- 4 large rice paper sheets
- Vegan mayonnaise
- Vegan cheese (optional)
- Vegan protein (tofu, tempeh, or seitan)
- Fresh herbs (cilantro, mint)
- Vegan fish sauce or soy sauce
- Chili slices (optional)

Directions

1. Preheat the oven to 350°F (175°C).
2. Spread vegan mayonnaise on each rice paper sheet.
3. Add vegan cheese, protein, and fresh herbs.
4. Bake for 5-7 minutes until crispy.
5. Drizzle with vegan fish sauce or soy sauce, and add chili slices for heat.
6. Enjoy your grilled rice paper snacks!

2 servings | 320 | 30 mins

Vegan Bánh Xèo (Savory Pancake)

These golden crispy pancakes are a Vietnamese delight. Stuffed with veggies and served with a tangy sauce.

Ingredients:

- For the Pancake:
 - 1 cup rice flour
 - 1 cup coconut milk
 - 1/2 cup water
 - 1/2 tsp turmeric powder
 - 1 cup bean sprouts
 - 1 cup mung bean
 - 2-3 green onions, chopped
 - Cooking oil
- For the Dipping Sauce:
 - Vegan fish sauce or soy sauce
 - Lime juice
 - Sugar
 - Garlic, minced
 - Chili slices (optional)

Directions

For the Pancake:
1. Mix rice flour, coconut milk, water, and turmeric powder until smooth.
2. Heat a non-stick pan, add oil, and pour in the batter.
3. Add bean sprouts, mung bean, and green onions.
4. Cook until crispy, then fold.
For the Dipping Sauce:
5. Mix vegan fish sauce, lime juice, sugar, garlic, and chili slices.
6. Dip and savor!

2 servings | 400 | 45 mins

Vegan Cơm Tấm Sườn Chay (Vegan "Pork" Rice)

A vegan twist on a beloved Vietnamese dish. Flavorful "pork" served over broken rice with a side of tangy sauce.

Ingredients:

- For the "Pork" Marinade:
 - 1 cup textured soy protein
 - 2 tbsp soy sauce
 - 1 tbsp oil
 - 1 tsp garlic powder
 - 1 tsp onion powder
 - 1 tsp paprika
- For the Broken Rice:
 - 1 cup broken rice
 - Vegan "pork" (marinated)
 - Fresh herbs (cilantro, mint)
 - Sliced cucumber
 - Pickled daikon and carrots
- For the Sauce:
 - Vegan fish sauce or soy sauce
 - Lime juice
 - Sugar
 - Garlic, minced

Directions

For the "Pork" Marinade:
1. Soak textured soy protein in hot water for 10 minutes, then drain.
2. Mix soy sauce, oil, and spices, then add the soy protein.
3. Marinate for 20 minutes and pan-fry until crispy.
For the Broken Rice:
4. Cook broken rice according to package instructions.
5. Serve with vegan "pork," herbs, cucumber, and pickles.
For the Sauce:
6. Mix vegan fish sauce, lime juice, sugar, and minced garlic.
7. Drizzle over the dish and enjoy!

4 servings | 120 | 25 mins

Vegan Gỏi Cuốn Chay (Vegan Spring Rolls)

Fresh and vibrant, these vegan spring rolls are filled with crisp veggies, herbs, and served with a zesty dipping sauce.

Ingredients:

- 8 rice paper wrappers
- Lettuce leaves
- Fresh herbs (cilantro, mint)
- Rice vermicelli, cooked and cooled
- Sliced cucumber
- Sliced bell peppers
- Sliced avocado
- Grated carrot
- Sliced tofu or tempeh
- Vegan hoisin-peanut dipping sauce
- Chili slices (optional)

Directions

1. Fill a large bowl with warm water. Dip each rice paper wrapper for a few seconds until pliable.
2. Lay on a clean surface and add lettuce, herbs, vermicelli, cucumber, bell peppers, avocado, carrot, and tofu or tempeh.
3. Roll tightly, tucking in the sides as you go.
4. Serve with hoisin-peanut sauce and chili slices.
5. Savor the freshness!

Chapter 9:
Authentic Vietnamese Dishes

4 servings 380 45 mins

Vegan Cá Kho Tộ (Braised "Fish" in Clay Pot)

Experience the savory depths of this traditional dish, now vegan-friendly. Braised "fish" in a clay pot with caramelized sauce.

Ingredients:

- 1 block of vegan "fish" (tofu or tempeh work well)
- 3 tbsp soy sauce
- 2 tbsp oil
- 1 onion, thinly sliced
- 3 cloves garlic, minced
- 2 tsp ginger, minced
- 3 tbsp brown sugar
- 2 tbsp vegan fish sauce or soy sauce
- 1 cup coconut water
- Fresh chili slices (optional)
- Fresh herbs (cilantro, Thai basil)

Directions

1. Cut the vegan "fish" into slices and marinate in soy sauce.
2. Heat oil in a clay pot and add onion, garlic, and ginger.
3. Add brown sugar and let it caramelize.
4. Add marinated "fish" and sear until golden.
5. Pour in vegan fish sauce, coconut water, and chili slices.
6. Simmer until the sauce thickens.
7. Garnish with fresh herbs.
8. Serve hot and enjoy the flavors!

4 servings | 280 | 30 mins

Vegan Bún Riêu (Crab Noodle Soup)

~~~~~~~~~~~~~

Dive into a bowl of vegan crab noodle soup, a comforting and flavorful dish that captures the essence of Vietnamese cuisine.

Ingredients:

- 8 oz vegan crabmeat or mushroom-based substitute
- 1 package rice vermicelli noodles
- 1 onion, chopped
- 3 cloves garlic, minced
- 2 tomatoes, diced
- 1/4 cup tomato paste
- 1/2 cup tofu, mashed
- 1 cup vegetable broth
- 1 tsp tamarind paste
- 1 tsp vegan shrimp paste (optional)
- Fresh herbs (cilantro, mint)
- Lime wedges
- Bean sprouts
- Chili slices (optional)

Directions

1. Cook rice vermicelli noodles according to package instructions.
2. In a pot, sauté onion and garlic until fragrant.
3. Add diced tomatoes and tomato paste, cooking until the tomatoes break down.
4. Stir in mashed tofu, vegetable broth, tamarind paste, and vegan shrimp paste (if using).
5. Simmer for 15 minutes.
6. Add vegan crabmeat and simmer for an additional 5 minutes.
7. Serve hot with noodles, fresh herbs, lime wedges, bean sprouts, and chili slices.
8. Enjoy your crab noodle soup!

Substitutions

Vegan crabmeat can be replaced with mushrooms or tofu.
Vegan shrimp paste is optional.
~~~~~~~~~~~~~

4 servings   320   45 mins

Vegan Bún Bò Huế (Spicy Noodle Soup)

A spicy and aromatic noodle soup that hails from Huế, Vietnam. Vegan-friendly and brimming with bold flavors.

Ingredients:

- 8 oz vegan beef slices or tofu
- 8 oz rice vermicelli noodles
- 1 onion, sliced
- 3 cloves garlic, minced
- 2 tbsp vegan lemongrass paste
- 2 tbsp vegan shrimp paste (optional)
- 1 tbsp chili oil (adjust to taste)
- 1 tsp paprika
- 1/2 tsp turmeric powder
- 6 cups vegetable broth
- Fresh herbs (cilantro, Thai basil, mint)
- Lime wedges
- Bean sprouts
- Sliced banana flowers (optional)
- Sliced bamboo shoots (optional)

Directions

1. Cook rice vermicelli noodles according to package instructions.
2. Sauté onion and garlic in a pot until fragrant.
3. Add vegan beef slices or tofu and brown them.
4. Stir in lemongrass paste, shrimp paste (if using), chili oil, paprika, and turmeric powder.
5. Pour in vegetable broth and simmer for 30 minutes.
6. Serve hot with noodles, fresh herbs, lime wedges, bean sprouts, banana flowers, and bamboo shoots.
7. Savor the spicy goodness!

Substitutions

Vegan beef slices can be replaced with tofu.
Vegan shrimp paste is optional.

4 servings | 320 | 40 mins

Vegan Cà Ri (Vietnamese Curry)

A comforting and aromatic Vietnamese curry made with an array of vegetables and tofu. Perfect for a cozy meal.

Ingredients:

- 1 block of tofu, cubed
- 1 onion, chopped
- 2 cloves garlic, minced
- 1 tbsp curry powder
- 1/2 tsp turmeric powder
- 1 can coconut milk
- 2 cups vegetable broth
- 1 carrot, sliced
- 1 potato, cubed
- 1 bell pepper, sliced
- 1 zucchini, sliced
- 1 cup green beans, chopped
- Fresh herbs (cilantro, mint)
- Lime wedges
- Cooked rice or baguette for serving

Directions

1. In a pot, sauté onion and garlic until fragrant.
2. Add curry powder and turmeric powder, stirring for a minute.
3. Pour in coconut milk and vegetable broth, bringing it to a simmer.
4. Add tofu, carrot, potato, bell pepper, zucchini, and green beans.
5. Simmer until the vegetables are tender.
6. Serve hot with fresh herbs, lime wedges, and your choice of rice or baguette.
7. Enjoy your comforting Vietnamese curry!

4 servings   280   35 mins

Vegan Mì Quảng (Turmeric Noodles)

Mì Quảng is a vibrant Vietnamese dish with turmeric-infused noodles, topped with an array of colorful ingredients.

Ingredients:

- 8 oz rice noodles
- 1 block of tofu, sliced
- 2 cloves garlic, minced
- 1 shallot, minced
- 2 tsp turmeric powder
- 2 tbsp oil
- 1 can coconut milk
- 1 cup vegetable broth
- 1/2 cup roasted peanuts, crushed
- Fresh herbs (cilantro, mint, Thai basil)
- Sliced banana flowers (optional)
- Lime wedges
- Bean sprouts
- Fresh chili slices (optional)

Substitutions

Sliced banana flowers can be omitted if unavailable.
Fresh chili slices are optional.

Directions

1. Cook rice noodles according to package instructions and set aside.
2. Sauté garlic and shallot in oil until fragrant.
3. Add turmeric powder and continue to cook.
4. Pour in coconut milk and vegetable broth, bringing it to a simmer.
5. Add sliced tofu and simmer for 10 minutes.
6. Serve noodles in bowls, topping with tofu, peanuts, herbs, banana flowers, lime wedges, bean sprouts, and chili slices if desired.
7. Savor the colorful flavors of Mì Quảng!

4 servings | 360 | 50 mins

Vegan Cơm Gà (Vegan "Chicken" Rice)

A vegan take on the classic Vietnamese chicken rice dish. Flavorful "chicken" served with fragrant rice and dipping sauce.

Ingredients:

- 1 block of vegan "chicken" (tofu, seitan, or tempeh)
- 1 cup jasmine rice
- 1/2 tsp ginger, minced
- 2 cloves garlic, minced
- 2 tbsp oil
- Vegan chicken seasoning (optional)
- Fresh herbs (cilantro, Thai basil)
- Sliced cucumber
- Lime wedges
- Vegan dipping sauce (hoisin-peanut sauce or vegan fish sauce)
- Fresh chili slices (optional)

Substitutions

Vegan chicken seasoning can be omitted if not available.
Fresh chili slices are optional.

Directions

1. Cook jasmine rice according to package instructions.
2. Slice the vegan "chicken" and marinate with ginger, garlic, and oil. Add vegan chicken seasoning if desired.
3. Grill or pan-fry until golden and aromatic.
4. Serve the "chicken" with jasmine rice, fresh herbs, sliced cucumber, lime wedges, and your choice of dipping sauce.
5. Garnish with fresh chili slices for an extra kick if desired.
6. Enjoy your vegan "chicken" rice!

4 servings   220   45 mins

Vegan Bánh Bao (Steamed Buns)

Soft and fluffy steamed buns filled with savory vegan ingredients. A delightful treat or a satisfying meal on its own.

Ingredients:

- 1 package of vegan steamed bun dough (or make your own)
- Vegan filling of choice (mushrooms, tofu, mock meats)
- Vegan hoisin sauce
- Fresh herbs (cilantro, Thai basil)
- Sliced cucumber
- Vegan fish sauce or soy sauce (for dipping)
- Fresh chili slices (optional)

Directions

1. Prepare the steamed bun dough according to package instructions or make your own.
2. Flatten small pieces of dough into circles, add your choice of vegan filling, and seal.
3. Steam the buns for 15-20 minutes until puffed and cooked.
4. Serve hot with vegan hoisin sauce, fresh herbs, sliced cucumber, and dipping sauce.
5. Garnish with fresh chili slices for an extra kick if desired.
6. Enjoy your vegan bánh bao!

4 servings   240   40 mins

Vegan Bánh Cuốn (Steamed Rice Rolls)

These delicate steamed rice rolls are filled with savory goodness and served with a flavorful dipping sauce.

Ingredients:

- 8 rice paper sheets
- Vegan filling (tofu, mushrooms, or tempeh)
- Vegan hoisin-peanut sauce or vegan fish sauce
- Fresh herbs (cilantro, Thai basil)
- Sliced cucumber
- Bean sprouts
- Fresh chili slices (optional)

Directions

1. Soak rice paper sheets in warm water until pliable.
2. Lay out a sheet and add your choice of vegan filling, herbs, cucumber, bean sprouts, and chili slices if desired.
3. Roll tightly, tucking in the sides as you go.
4. Serve with your preferred dipping sauce.
5. Savor the delicate flavors of bánh cuốn!

4 servings | 340 | 30 mins

Vegan Cơm Rang (Fried Rice)

A quick and satisfying Vietnamese fried rice, packed with veggies and savory vegan protein.

Ingredients:

- 2 cups cooked jasmine rice, cooled
- 1 cup mixed vegetables (peas, carrots, corn, bell peppers)
- 1 cup vegan protein (tofu, tempeh, or mock meats), diced
- 2 cloves garlic, minced
- 2 tbsp soy sauce
- 1 tbsp oil
- Fresh herbs (cilantro, Thai basil)
- Lime wedges
- Sliced cucumber
- Fresh chili slices (optional)

Directions

1. Heat oil in a pan and sauté garlic until fragrant.
2. Add vegan protein and cook until lightly browned.
3. Add mixed vegetables and continue to stir-fry.
4. Stir in cooked jasmine rice and soy sauce, ensuring even distribution.
5. Cook until everything is well combined and heated through.
6. Serve hot with fresh herbs, lime wedges, sliced cucumber, and chili slices if desired.
7. Enjoy your cơm rang!

2 servings   340   25 mins

Vegan Bánh Mì (Vietnamese Sandwich)

The classic Vietnamese sandwich, made vegan! Layers of flavor in a baguette, perfect for a quick and satisfying meal.

Ingredients:

- 1 vegan baguette
- Vegan mayonnaise
- Vegan pâté
- Vegan protein (tofu, tempeh, seitan, or mock meats)
- Fresh vegetables (lettuce, cucumber, tomato)
- Vegan cheese slices (optional)
- Pickles
- Soy sauce or hot sauce (optional)

Directions

1. Slice the baguette in half and lightly toast it.
2. Spread vegan mayonnaise and pâté on both sides.
3. Layer with vegan protein, fresh veggies, vegan cheese, and pickles.
4. Close the sandwich and enjoy this savory delight!

Chapter 10:
Fusion Flavors

2 tacos   320   30 mins

Vegan Bánh Mì Tacos

A playful twist on the classic Bánh Mì sandwich, now in taco form.

Ingredients:

- 4 small tortillas
- 1 cup sliced tofu
- 1/2 cup pickled daikon and carrot
- 1/4 cup cucumber slices
- 2 tbsp vegan mayo
- 2 tbsp hoisin sauce
- Fresh cilantro leaves

Directions

1. Warm the tortillas in a pan.
2. In a separate pan, sauté tofu until golden.
3. Assemble tacos with tofu, pickled veggies, cucumber, mayo, hoisin, and cilantro.
4. Enjoy!

Substitutions

- Use tempeh instead of tofu
- Use sriracha instead of hoisin
- Add jalapeños for extra kick

1 pizza   450   40 mins

Vegan Bánh Mì Pizza

Pizza meets Vietnamese flavors in this delectable fusion creation.

Ingredients:

- 1 pizza dough
- 1/2 cup vegan mayo
- 2 cloves garlic (minced)
- 1 cup shredded carrots
- 1 cup sliced cucumber
- 1 cup marinated tofu
- 1/4 cup fresh cilantro leaves
- 2 tbsp hoisin sauce

Directions

1. Preheat oven to 425°F (220°C).
2. Roll out pizza dough.
3. Spread vegan mayo and garlic as the base.
4. Add carrots, cucumber, and tofu.
5. Bake until crust is golden.
6. Drizzle with hoisin and garnish with cilantro.
7. Slice and savor.

Substitutions

- Use vegan cheese for added richness
- Add bean sprouts for extra crunch

1 burger   380   40 mins

Vegan Pho Burger

A burger infused with the fragrant essence of Vietnamese Pho.

Ingredients:

- 1 vegan burger patty
- 1 burger bun
- 1 cup vegetable broth
- 1/2 cup cooked rice noodles
- 1/4 cup bean sprouts
- 1/4 cup fresh basil leaves
- Sriracha to taste

Directions

1. Cook the burger patty as desired.
2. Warm the bun in the oven.
3. Heat vegetable broth.
4. Assemble burger with noodles, bean sprouts, basil, and Sriracha.
5. Pour broth on the side for dipping.
6. Bite into Pho-inspired bliss.

Substitutions

- Use a gluten-free bun for a gluten-free option
- Add sliced jalapeños for heat

1 burrito   280   25 mins

Vegan Spring Roll Burrito

The freshness of Vietnamese spring rolls wrapped in a burrito.

Ingredients:

- 1 large tortilla
- 1 cup cooked rice vermicelli
- 1/2 cup shredded lettuce
- 1/2 cup julienned cucumber
- 1/4 cup sliced avocado
- 1/4 cup fresh mint leaves
- Vegan peanut sauce

Directions

1. Soften tortilla in a hot pan.
2. Lay out rice vermicelli, lettuce, cucumber, avocado, and mint.
3. Drizzle with peanut sauce.
4. Roll it up tightly.
5. Slice and serve.

Substitutions

- Add crispy tofu for extra protein
- Use almond butter sauce instead of peanut sauce for a different twist

2 sliders   240   20 mins

Vegan Tofu Bánh Mì Sliders

Tiny sandwiches bursting with Vietnamese flavor.

Ingredients:

- 2 mini slider buns
- 1/2 cup marinated tofu slices
- 1/4 cup pickled daikon and carrot
- 2 tbsp vegan mayo
- 2 tbsp chopped cilantro
- Sliced jalapeños (optional)

Directions

1. Toast slider buns in a pan.
2. Assemble with tofu, pickled veggies, mayo, cilantro, and jalapeños if desired.
3. Serve hot and enjoy the mini delights.

Substitutions

- Use tempeh instead of tofu for a different texture
- Add sriracha for heat

 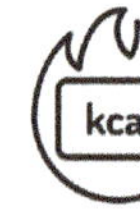 

6 rolls | 320 | 35 mins

Vegan Vietnamese-Inspired Sushi

Sushi with a Vietnamese twist, packed with fresh ingredients.

Ingredients:

- 6 nori seaweed sheets
- 1 cup cooked sushi rice
- 1/2 cup julienned cucumber
- 1/2 cup julienned carrot
- 1/4 cup sliced avocado
- 1/4 cup fresh mint leaves
- Vegan soy sauce for dipping

Directions

1. Place a bamboo sushi rolling mat on a clean surface.
2. Lay down a sheet of plastic wrap on the mat.
3. Place a nori sheet on the plastic wrap.
4. Spread sushi rice on the nori, leaving a border.
5. Add cucumber, carrot, avocado, and mint.
6. Roll tightly using the mat.
7. Slice into bite-sized pieces.
8. Dip in soy sauce and savor.

Substitutions

- Add marinated tofu for extra protein
- Use gluten-free soy sauce for a gluten-free option

2 bowls · 280 · 45 mins

Vegan Pho-Style Ramen

A fusion of Vietnamese Pho and Japanese Ramen in one comforting bowl.

Ingredients:

- 2 servings of ramen noodles
- 4 cups vegetable broth
- 1 cup sliced mushrooms
- 1/2 cup bean sprouts
- 1/4 cup fresh basil leaves
- Lime wedges and Sriracha for garnish

Directions

1. Cook ramen noodles according to package instructions.
2. In a separate pot, heat vegetable broth and add mushrooms.
3. Divide cooked noodles into bowls.
4. Pour broth over noodles and top with bean sprouts and basil.
5. Serve with lime wedges and Sriracha.

Substitutions

- Add sliced tofu for extra protein
- Use rice noodles for a gluten-free option

2 tacos   350   35 mins

Vegan Bánh Xèo Tacos

A tantalizing fusion of Vietnamese Bánh Xèo and Mexican tacos.

Ingredients:

- 4 small tortillas
- 1 cup rice flour batter (for Bánh Xèo)
- 1/2 cup mung bean sprouts
- 1/4 cup sliced mushrooms
- 1/4 cup sliced bell peppers
- Vegan fish sauce for dipping

Directions

1. Heat a non-stick pan and pour a ladle of rice flour batter to make a thin crepe (Bánh Xèo).
2. Add mushrooms and bell peppers, fold in half, and cook until crispy.
3. Warm tortillas in a pan.
4. Fill with Bánh Xèo, bean sprouts, and serve with vegan fish sauce.

Substitutions

- Use chickpea flour for a gluten-free batter
- Add sliced jalapeños for heat

 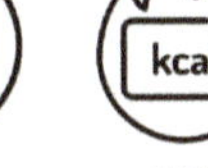 

2 servings | 180 | 15 mins

Vegan Pho-Inspired Salad

All the flavors of Pho in a refreshing salad form.

Ingredients:

- 4 cups mixed greens
- 1 cup cooked rice noodles
- 1/2 cup bean sprouts
- 1/4 cup fresh basil leaves
- 1/4 cup sliced radishes
- Vegan Pho broth dressing

Directions

1. Toss mixed greens and cooked rice noodles in a bowl.
2. Top with bean sprouts, basil, and radishes.
3. Drizzle with Pho broth dressing.
4. Dive into the vibrant flavors.

Substitutions

- Add marinated tempeh or tofu for extra protein
- Use zucchini noodles for a low-carb option

1 burrito   340   30 mins

Vegan Bánh Mì Burrito

A hearty fusion of Vietnamese Bánh Mì and a burrito.

Ingredients:

- 1 large tortilla
- 1/2 cup cooked jasmine rice
- 1/4 cup sliced tofu
- 1/4 cup pickled daikon and carrot
- 2 tbsp vegan mayo
- 2 tbsp hoisin sauce
- Fresh cilantro leaves

Directions

1. Soften tortilla in a hot pan.
2. Lay out cooked rice, tofu, pickled veggies, mayo, hoisin, and cilantro.
3. Roll it up into a burrito.
4. Slice and savor the fusion.

Substitutions

- Use brown rice for added nutrition
- Add sriracha for extra heat

Chapter 11:
Sweet Endings

4 servings   200   30 mins

Vegan Chè Ba Màu (Three-Color Dessert)

A delightful Vietnamese dessert symbolizing harmony and balance.

Ingredients:

- 1/2 cup mung beans (cooked and mashed)
- 1/2 cup red bean paste
- 1/2 cup green pandan jelly
- 1/4 cup coconut milk
- 1/4 cup sugar
- Crushed ice

Directions

1. In serving glasses, layer the mashed mung beans, red bean paste, and pandan jelly.
2. Top with crushed ice.
3. Drizzle with coconut milk and sugar.
4. Enjoy the vibrant layers of sweetness.

Substitutions

- Use different fruit jellies for variety
- Substitute coconut milk with almond milk for a lighter option

12 balls   180   45 mins

Vegan Bánh Cam (Orange Glutinous Rice Balls)

These golden rice balls are a traditional Vietnamese sweet treat.

Ingredients:

- 1 cup glutinous rice flour
- 1/4 cup orange sweet potato (mashed)
- 1/4 cup sugar
- 1/4 cup coconut milk
- Cooking oil for frying

Directions

1. In a bowl, mix glutinous rice flour, mashed sweet potato, and sugar until dough forms.
2. Shape into balls.
3. Heat oil and deep-fry until golden.
4. Drain and serve the crispy, sweet Bánh Cam.

Substitutions

- Add a pinch of cinnamon for extra flavor
- Dust with powdered sugar for added sweetness

8 slices   280   50 mins

Vegan Bánh Bò Nướng (Pandan Honeycomb Cake)

Normal

A fragrant and spongy cake infused with pandan and coconut.

Ingredients:

- 1 cup rice flour
- 1/2 cup tapioca starch
- 1/2 cup sugar
- 1/2 cup coconut milk
- 1/4 cup pandan juice
- 1 tsp baking powder
- Cooking oil for greasing

Substitutions

- Use vanilla extract if pandan juice is unavailable
- Top with toasted coconut flakes for extra texture

Directions

1. Mix rice flour, tapioca starch, sugar, coconut milk, pandan juice, and baking powder until smooth.
2. Grease a baking pan.
3. Pour batter and steam for 45 minutes.
4. Cool and slice into honeycomb-shaped pieces.
5. Savor the aromatic delight.

6 servings | 220 | 40 mins

Vegan Bánh Flan (Creme Caramel)

A creamy and caramel-infused dessert that melts in your mouth.

Ingredients:

- 1/2 cup sugar (for caramel)
- 1 cup coconut milk
- 1/2 cup sugar
- 1/4 cup silken tofu
- 1 tsp vanilla extract
- Pinch of salt

Directions

1. In a pan, melt sugar until golden for caramel.
2. Pour into ramekins.
3. Blend coconut milk, sugar, tofu, vanilla, and salt until smooth.
4. Pour mixture over caramel.
5. Steam for 30 minutes.
6. Chill, then invert and serve the luscious Bánh Flan.

Substitutions

- Use almond milk instead of coconut milk for a nuttier flavor
- Substitute tofu with cashews for a creamier texture

9 squares | 250 | 50 mins

Vegan Bánh Gan (Cassava Cake)

A dense and chewy cake made from cassava, a tropical delight.

Ingredients:

- 2 cups grated cassava
- 1 cup coconut milk
- 1/2 cup sugar
- 1/4 cup shredded coconut
- 1/4 cup vegan condensed milk
- Pinch of salt

Directions

1. Mix grated cassava, coconut milk, sugar, shredded coconut, vegan condensed milk, and salt in a bowl.
2. Pour into a greased baking dish.
3. Bake at 350°F (175°C) for 40 minutes until golden.
4. Slice and enjoy the cassava goodness.

Substitutions

- Add a layer of jackfruit for a tropical twist
- Drizzle with maple syrup for added sweetness

8 slices — 220 — 45 mins

Vegan Bánh Kem Chuối (Banana Cake)

Easy

Moist and flavorful, this banana cake is a crowd-pleaser.

Ingredients:

- 1 cup mashed ripe bananas
- 1/2 cup sugar
- 1/4 cup coconut oil
- 1/4 cup coconut milk
- 1 cup all-purpose flour
- 1 tsp baking powder
- 1/2 tsp baking soda
- Pinch of salt

Directions

1. Mix mashed bananas, sugar, coconut oil, and coconut milk in a bowl.
2. In another bowl, whisk flour, baking powder, baking soda, and salt.
3. Combine wet and dry ingredients.
4. Bake in a greased pan at 350°F (175°C) for 35-40 minutes.
5. Slice and relish the banana goodness.

Substitutions

- Add chopped walnuts for a delightful crunch
- Top with vegan cream cheese frosting for extra indulgence

8 slices 320 60 mins

Vegan Bánh Tét (Sticky Rice Cake)

A traditional Vietnamese New Year's treat, filled with nostalgia.

Ingredients:

- 2 cups glutinous rice
- 1/2 cup mung bean paste
- 1/4 cup coconut milk
- Banana leaves for wrapping
- Cooking twine

Substitutions

- Add a layer of vegan sausage for a savory twist
- Use parchment paper if banana leaves are unavailable

Directions

1. Soak glutinous rice in water for 4 hours, then drain.
2. Mix rice with coconut milk.
3. Lay out banana leaves and place a layer of rice, mung bean paste, and another layer of rice.
4. Roll tightly, wrap in banana leaves, and tie with twine.
5. Steam for 1 hour.
6. Slice and celebrate the tradition.

6 servings   280   40 mins

Vegan Bánh Tiramisu

A Vietnamese twist on the classic Italian dessert.

Ingredients:

- 1 cup brewed coffee
- 1/4 cup sugar
- 1/4 cup rum (optional)
- 1 cup vegan cream cheese
- 1/2 cup powdered sugar
- 1/4 cup coconut milk
- Vegan ladyfingers
- Cocoa powder for dusting

Directions

1. Combine brewed coffee, sugar, and rum (if using).
2. In a separate bowl, mix vegan cream cheese, powdered sugar, and coconut milk until smooth.
3. Dip ladyfingers in coffee mixture and layer in a dish.
4. Spread cream cheese mixture over ladyfingers.
5. Repeat layers.
6. Dust with cocoa powder.
7. Chill and savor the Vietnamese Tiramisu.

Substitutions

- Use espresso for a stronger coffee flavor
- Substitute rum with coffee liqueur for a twist

4 servings   180   35 mins

Super Easy

Vegan Chè Thập Cẩm (Mixed Sweet Soup)

A delightful medley of textures and flavors in a sweet soup.

Ingredients:

- 1/4 cup mung beans (cooked)
- 1/4 cup black-eyed peas (cooked)
- 1/4 cup red beans (cooked)
- 1/4 cup tapioca pearls (cooked)
- 1/4 cup coconut milk
- 1/4 cup sugar
- A pinch of salt

Directions

1. Cook mung beans, black-eyed peas, red beans, and tapioca pearls separately until soft.
2. In a pot, combine all cooked ingredients, coconut milk, sugar, and salt.
3. Simmer until well combined.
4. Serve warm or chilled, relishing the mix of textures and flavors.

Substitutions

- Add sweet potato for added sweetness
- Use almond milk for a lighter version

4 servings   250   25 mins

Vegan Kem Dâu (Strawberry Ice Cream)

Creamy and luscious strawberry ice cream for a sweet ending.

Ingredients:

- 2 cups frozen strawberries
- 1/2 cup coconut milk
- 1/4 cup sugar
- 1 tsp vanilla extract
- Pinch of salt

Directions

1. Blend frozen strawberries, coconut milk, sugar, vanilla extract, and salt until smooth.
2. Pour into an ice cream maker and churn according to the manufacturer's instructions.
3. Freeze until firm.
4. Scoop and savor the homemade strawberry delight.

Substitutions

- Add chocolate chips for a delightful twist
- Substitute strawberries with other frozen fruits for variety

We need your support

As we conclude our flavorful journey through the "Vietnamese Vegan Cookbook," I want to extend my heartfelt appreciation to you, the adventurous souls who've explored the world of plant-based Vietnamese cuisine with us. Together, we've delved into the intricate tapestry of flavors that make Vietnamese food so extraordinary.

Before we bid adieu to this culinary adventure, I have a humble request to make. In the world of small publishers like us, reviews are the currency of connection, the lifeblood that keeps our culinary creations alive and thriving. They're as elusive as the perfect pho broth.

If you've found inspiration in our collection of Vietnamese vegan recipes, if you've marveled at the simplicity of sourcing ingredients and creating authentic meals, I kindly ask for your support. Please take a moment to return to the app or website where you acquired this book, where you'll discover that precious review button. There, you can bestow upon us a rating and share a brief sentence or two about your experience.

Your review isn't just a comment; it's a bridge. It guides fellow culinary explorers to these pages, and it fortifies our mission to make Vietnamese vegan cooking accessible and delectable. Every review you leave is like a fragrant herb that flavors our passion for plant-based Vietnamese cuisine, and we read each one with genuine appreciation and excitement.

And if, by any chance, you've come across a minor hiccup or oversight along the way, please understand that we've poured our heart and soul into crafting this culinary adventure. Despite our unwavering commitment, even the most dedicated chefs can sometimes encounter bumps in the road. Your understanding is the fish sauce that adds depth to our culinary journey.

As we conclude this Vietnamese odyssey, I want to thank you once again for being a part of it. Your reviews, your support, and your presence here have made this culinary voyage all the more enriching.

Now, as you return to your kitchen, inspired by the allure of Vietnamese vegan cuisine, let's continue to savor the art of plant-based cooking. Until we meet again in the fragrant embrace of Vietnamese herbs and flavors, stay curious, keep experimenting, and relish the joy of every Vietnamese-inspired creation. Your culinary adventure continues, and we're profoundly grateful to have been a part of it.